This catalogue of design for theatre
and performance is a companion to
2D|3D, an international exhibition
which opened at the Millennium
Galleries, Sheffield, in October 2002.

The exhibition shows work executed,
between 1999 and 2002, by designers
born or based in the UK.
The catalogue illustrates the work of
these designers in opera, dance,
drama and event making.
It includes designs for set, costume
and lighting as well as the designs of
performance spaces.

Neither the exhibition nor the
catalogue is a comprehensive survey
of the period. Both are a celebration of
the diversity and richness of current
theatre practice in the UK.

2D|3D

Design for theatre

and performance

Compiled by

Peter Ruthven Hall

and Kate Burnett

The Society of British Theatre Designers is deeply grateful to all the sponsors, from private individuals to large organisations, who have made this exhibition, its catalogue and programme of educational events possible. Sincere thanks are due to:

Published in Great Britain by
The Society of British
Theatre Designers
47 Bermondsey Street
London SE1 3XT

Registered Charity No: 800638

Text copyright © 2002

ISBN 0-9529309-2-7

British Library Cataloguing in Publication Data: a catalogue record of this book is available from the British Library

Design and Typography
by Simon Head

Edited by Keith Allen
and Phyllida Shaw

Photography of Section page model by Tim Crocker

Printed by Spiderweb

Photographs and illustrations are by the contributing designer unless otherwise stated.

Information in this catalogue has been provided by contributing designers and is published in good faith.

The Arts Council of England

The D'Oyly Carte Charitable Trust
Gerriets Great Britain Ltd
John Lewis Partnership Plc
The Mackintosh Foundation

Ambassador Theatre Group
The Arts Club Charitable Trust
Arts Team at RHWL
Association of Lighting Designers
Alan Ayckbourn
Maria Björnson
Bower Wood Production Services
Brilliant Stages Ltd
Bob Crowley
Ann Curtis
Delstar Engineering Ltd
Flint Hire & Supply
John Gunter
J & C Joel Ltd
Lee Filters Ltd
Library Theatre Manchester
Lite Structures (GB) Ltd
Northern Light
Philip L Edwards Theatre Lighting
Philips Lighting
Roscolab Ltd
Souvenir Scenic Studios
The Stage Newspaper Ltd
Stage One
Stage Technologies Ltd
Steeldeck UK
Stephen Pyle Workshops
Talbot Designs Ltd
Terry Murphy Scenery
Mark Thompson
University of Derby
University of Leeds, Bretton Hall
Anthony Ward
White Light Ltd
White Light (North) Ltd

Thanks are also due to the following for their inspiration, commitment and practical help:

David Adams; Howard Bird, Executive Director, ABTT; Sean Crowley and Andrea Montag, design schools exhibition, Royal Welsh College of Music and Drama; Jenny Straker, Administrator, ABTT; Simon Thomas-Colquhoun, Technical Director; Sophie Tyrrell, education notes; Colin Winslow, SBTD website; Gary Withers; the staff of Sheffield Galleries & Museums Trust.

2D>3D draws on the resources and membership of the following organisations which include theatre designers, technicians and architects:

The Society of British
Theatre Designers

The Association of British
Theatre Technicians

The Association of
Lighting Designers

Equity Register of Designers

Society of Theatre Consultants

Patrons:
Judi Dench DBE
Richard Eyre KBE
Beryl Grey DBE
Jocelyn Herbert
Nicholas Hytner
Bruce McLean
Brian McMaster CBE
Adrian Noble
Trevor Nunn CBE

In memory of Terry Bennet

Millennium Galleries

THE
ARTS
COUNCIL
OF ENGLAND

Contents

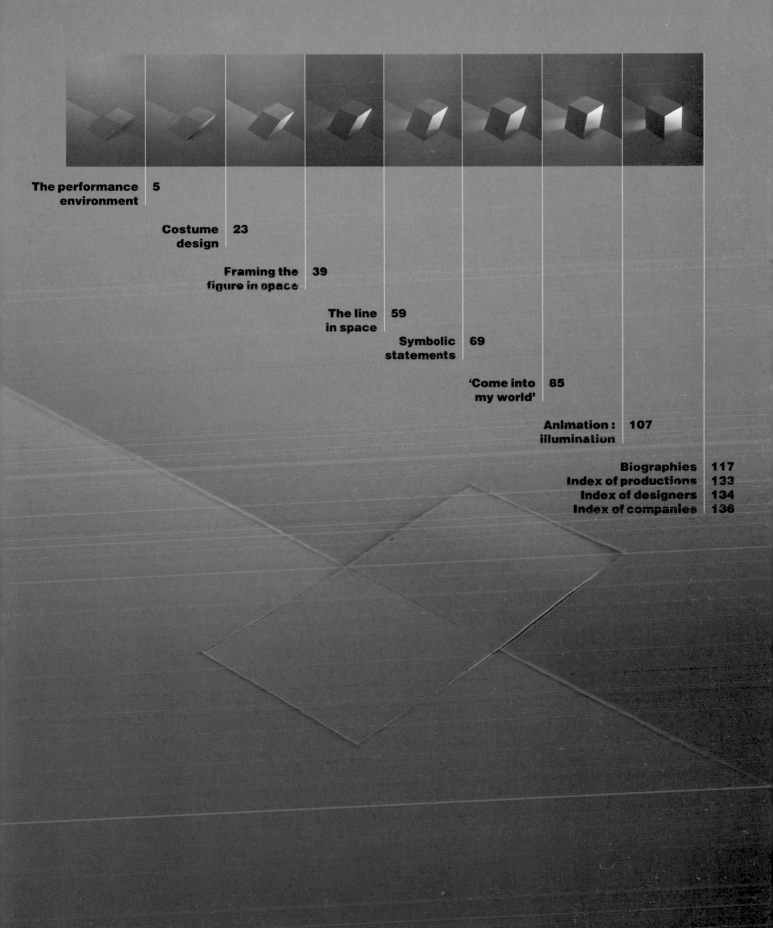

Introduction

This national exhibition of design for performance is the third themed and curated exhibition mounted by the Society of British Theatre Designers. It provides an insight into the innovation and imagination of British designers now working all over the world.

'The designer thinks in terms of the fourth dimension, the passage of time, not the stage picture, but the stage moving picture,' wrote Peter Brook in The Shifting Point: 40 years of exploration 1946-1987 (Methuen). So why is our focus on 2D>3D?

In preparing this exhibition we were aware that the designs, in the form of drawings, models, computer visualisations and even actual costumes and props would be incomplete. They lack the coalescing moment of performance in which meaning is made in the perceptions of the audience.

Designers are sometimes asked: 'Do you make models as mementoes of the production?' Well no, we don't. Models are an important part of the design process, to both the conception of a production and in communicating with the creative teams who realise the design for performance. This question is important because it highlights the invisibility of the labour intensive process of designing sets, costumes, lighting and projection for performance.

By taking 2D>3D as its theme, the exhibition demonstrates many individual approaches to design. It connects our imagination and experience as designers, working out of different cultural and ethnic backgrounds, with the imagination and experience of viewers, in all their diversity, in the journey from mind to page, from computer screen to performance space. It is a theme that naturally suggests the many practical and technical aspects of design for performance and the variety of working processes.

In 2D, ideas are worked up in sketches, storyboards and montages, as well as on computer, in virtual visualisation, image capture and manipulation. The point at which design ideas move into 3D varies from one designer to another. Some make preliminary models at a smaller scale, such as 1:100 or 1:50, or work through several white card versions at 1:25. Others start in 3D, working in rehearsal, developing ideas with performers in 'real space'.

Costume designs, in the form of sketches, colour schemes, charts, pattern and detail drawings are generally translated into 3D at life size, either in calico toiles or the actual fabric. Technical drawings on paper or computer, however, translate the model, drawing or virtual image for full-scale construction. Many designers problem-solve using 2D and 3D methods in tandem. Young designers are often employed to develop another designer's ideas through model making and technical drawing.

The practical considerations of design for performance interweave with conceptual concerns. Developing structures and costuming the figure involve considering their relationship with the space around them.
• The proscenium arch may be used as a picture frame, presenting the space within it, but it can also be part of a dynamic thrust stage. How do 3D set structures relate to the (3D) performer in spaces in-the-round, traverse or three-sided thrust stages? How do these spaces frame or present the performer?
• In found spaces, audiences experience the architectural space around them as part of the performance, in promenade or on a guided journey.
• In the abstract space of line, plane and colour, figure and space relate to each other sculpturally, described by light. Revealing or concealing, lighting governs the illusions created by both 2D painting and 3D structures.
• In the geography of a stage space, landmarks are created by furniture and other structures. Designs for outdoor performances and events exploit natural landmarks in the relationship of the environment to human scale.

Much of the work presented here could sit comfortably in more than one of the categories chosen to explore the 2D>3D theme. It also defies categorisation as either Art or Design. For as well as being a blueprint for full-scale realisation, each design is a unique artwork made by one artist-designer, as well as the product of a particular set of circumstances and individuals.

Presenting designs for 3D performance in the 2D format of the page (or screen) inevitably influences our reading of the image. Ultimately it is for the viewers and readers to animate the designers' 2D images and 3D models into the fourth dimension of their mind's eye.

Kate Burnett and Peter Ruthven Hall

The performance environment

Perhaps the single greatest influence on a performance is the environment in which it takes place. Where did you last see a performance: in a theatre, a disused factory, a park, a playground, a church? Wherever it was, the challenge for the designer was to make the connection between the space, the performance and the audience.

This section contains a mixture of design for new spaces,[1] for renovated spaces[2] and for temporary, found spaces. The Almeida finds a temporary home in a bus depot in Kings Cross, while its permanent home (a former chapel) is being renovated. The National Lottery has helped to fund new buildings as well as the upgrading of existing spaces to contemporary technical standards.

Also featured here are designs which reconfigure an existing theatre space, and reorder the performer-audience relationship[3, 4]. Repertory companies across the country regularly mount summer productions in a local park.[5] Derelict hospitals, streets, doorways and underpasses all inspire designs for performance.[6]

In designing for found spaces, sketches and storyboards are often the only prelude to working in the space. Increasingly, some form of digital information is used. This may be in the form of photographic collages against which moments are designed or of digitally captured patterns and textures applied to digitally designed structures, for realisation at full scale.

In effective computer visualisations, the information of a new building, performance space or set design may be experienced from a variety of audience and performer viewpoints.[7]

1 Keith Williams Architects, Unicorn Theatre p20
2 Haworth Tompkins, Royal Court Theatre, p10
3 Stefanos Lazaridis, ENO Italian Opera Season p12
4 Pamela Howard, La Celestina p14
5 Gabriella Csanyi-Wills, A Midsummer Night's Dream p17
6 Fred Meller, Ghost Ward p15,
   Louise Ann Wilson, Mapping the Edge p21
7 Roma Patel, Skeletons of Fish p22, Ian Teague, Henry V p22

Avery Associates

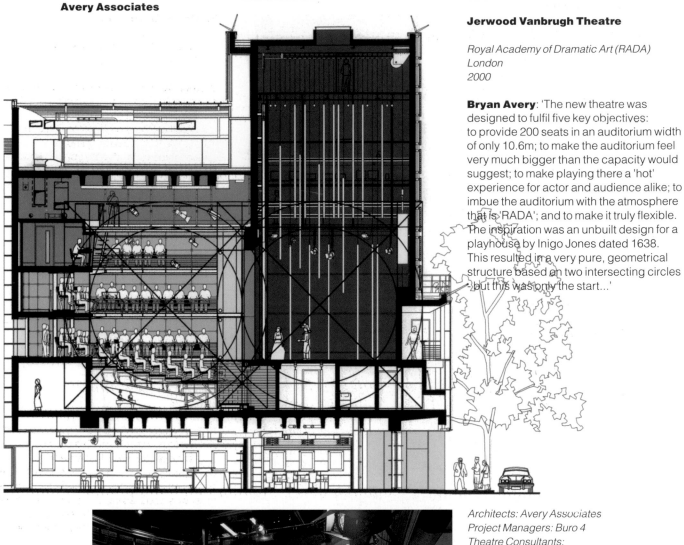

Jerwood Vanbrugh Theatre

Royal Academy of Dramatic Art (RADA)
London
2000

Bryan Avery: 'The new theatre was designed to fulfil five key objectives: to provide 200 seats in an auditorium width of only 10.6m; to make the auditorium feel very much bigger than the capacity would suggest; to make playing there a 'hot' experience for actor and audience alike; to imbue the auditorium with the atmosphere that is 'RADA'; and to make it truly flexible. The inspiration was an unbuilt design for a playhouse by Inigo Jones dated 1638. This resulted in a very pure, geometrical structure based on two intersecting circles – but this was only the start...'

Architects: Avery Associates
Project Managers: Buro 4
Theatre Consultants:
Theatre Projects Consultants
Acoustic Engineers:
Paul Gillieron Acoustic Design
M&E Engineers: Roger Preston & Partners
Structural Engineers: Ove Arup & Partners
Access Consultants: All Clear Designs
Quantity Surveyors: Davis Langdon & Everest
Main Contractor: Laing Construction
Specialist Subcontractors: Integrated Video
Communications Ltd, LT Projects, Mole
Richardson, Telestage Associates,
Mirage Seating
Photographer: Mark Tupper

Jennie Norman

The Phoenix Theatre

Drama Department, Bristol University
1999/2002

Jennie Norman: 'This reconstruction of a candlelit Jacobean playhouse is based on a set of drawings by Inigo Jones (unidentified, but possibly The Phoenix, 1617). The four-sided audience relationship in this intimate space allows no spectator to be more than 7.3m from an actor at the centre of the stage. Spectators and actors likened entering the stage to "walking into the arms of the audience.'

Director: Martin White
Set Designer: Jennie Norman
Lighting Designer: Rod Terry
Construction: Quentin Nichols/Tim Gardener
Photographer: John Adler

Will Bowen

The Loft Theatre

Transformation Season 2002
The National Theatre - London
May 2002

Will Bowen: 'The National Theatre required a cheap, temporary, re-usable space for an audience of 100. With its low ceilings, concrete walls and purple, carpeted floor, the exhibition area of the Lyttelton Theatre circle foyer was about as imperfect as you can get. But with a little ingenuity, the space was transformed and the Loft Theatre was born.'

Theatre Designer and Consultant: Will Bowen
Acoustic Consultant: Richard Cowell, Arup Acoustics
Structural Engineer: Brian Horton, Flint & Neill Partnership
Photographer: Philip Carter

Nathalie Maury

Hampstead Theatre

London
Opening 2003

Nathalie Maury: 'Commissioned to create a visualisation for the new theatre, I made a 3D computer model, using the architects' design. I worked closely with Jenny Topper and James Williams, who used the model to explore the space, and position themselves in the auditorium. I provided a new perspective to test and refine the technical attributes of the design.'

Architect: Bennetts Associates
Theatre Consultant: Tech Plan
Visualisation: Nathalie Maury
Artistic Director: Jenny Topper
Executive Director: James Williams

Paul Brown

The Tempest
William Shakespeare
Almeida - London
December 2000

Platonov
Anton Chekhov
Almeida Kings Cross - London
August 2001

King Lear
William Shakespeare
Almeida Kings Cross - London
January 2002

Paul Brown: 'Over a period of two years I worked with the director Jonathon Kent on a series of plays by Shakespeare and Chekhov for the Almeida Theatre.
The valedictory nature of *The Tempest* (left) made it a fitting choice for the final production in the old Almeida theatre.
We partially demolished the theatre and flooded it in three metres of water. The resulting waterlogged landscape helped to blur the boundary between illusion and reality. Techniques employed at the derelict bus garage in Kings Cross ranged from creating a slice of Russian landscape within the confines of a room
(*Platonov*, above right), to the conceit of setting up and destroying panelled walls within the concrete shell (*King Lear*, below right).

Director: Jonathon Kent
Set and Costume Designer: Paul Brown
Lighting Designer: Mark Henderson
Assistant Designer: Ros Coombes
Photographer: Ivan Kyncl

Haworth Tompkins

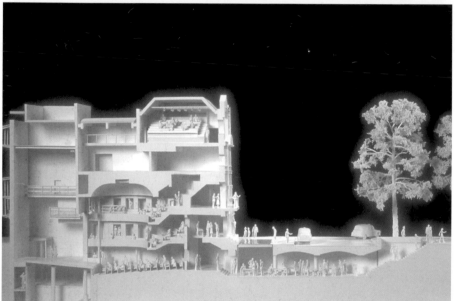

Royal Court Theatre

London
1996 - 2000

Steven Tompkins: 'The remodelling of
this famous theatre doubled the space
available for audience, actors and staff.
Technical systems were upgraded and full
accessibility achieved for the first time.
In making these radical alterations we
adopted an archaeological approach to
the building, emphasising the evolution of
past changes and revealing the history of
the theatre as a continuous process of
change. Materials were selected for their
ability to mellow with use and to
complement the found surfaces of the old
structure. The beautiful auditorium (400
seats) was allowed to maintain continuity,
reinterpreted rather than reinvented.
Spaces both front and back of house were
designed to support the work on stage in
an unassertive but stimulating way.'

Architect: Haworth Tompkins
Theatre Consultant:
Theatre Projects Consultants
Artist Collaborator: Antoni Malinowski
Structural Engineer: Price and Myers
Environmental Engineer: Max Fordham LLP
Acoustician: Paul Gillieron Acoustic Design
Cost consultant: Citex
Construction Manager: Schal
Photographer: Andy Chopping

Almeida @ Gainsborough Studios

London
2000

Steven Tompkins: 'This temporary
theatre was designed for two Shakespeare
productions (*Richard II* and *Coriolanus*) in
a disused power station in Shoreditch.
We attempted the most direct
transformation possible, demolishing a
floor to create a single, huge courtyard
space (800 seats) dominated by Paul
Brown's architectural "set". Front and back
of house facilities were provided with the
minimum means; scaffolding, trestles and
unfinished plasterboard being the sole
materials offered against the texture of the
found space, lit with builders' lights and
roughly patched against the weather.
Our preoccupation was to keep that sense
of benign trespass and danger on entering
a derelict building.'

Architect. Haworth Tompkins
Partner in charge: Steve Tompkins
Structural Engineer: Alan Conisbee Associates
Environmental Engineer: Max Fordham LLP
Acoustician: Paul Gillieron Acoustic Design
Construction Manager and Cost Consultant:
Citex
Photographer: Andy Chopping

Anthony Lamble

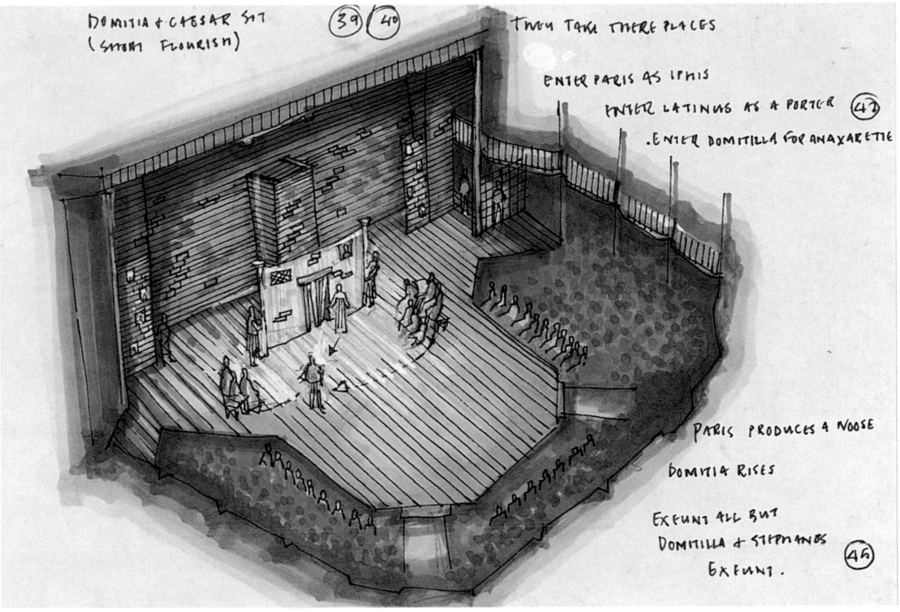

[handwritten annotations on sketch:]
DOMITIA & CAESAR SIT (SHORT FLOURISH) (39)(40)
THEY TAKE THERE PLACES
ENTER PARIS AS IPHIS
ENTER LATINUS AS A PORTER (41)
ENTER DOMITILLA FOR ANAXARETIE
PARIS PRODUCES A NOOSE
DOMITIA RISES
EXEUNT ALL BUT DOMITILLA & STEPHANOS (46) EXEUNT.

The Roman Actor
Philip Massinger

Royal Shakespeare Company
The Swan Theatre - Stratford-upon-Avon
May 2002

Anthony Lamble: 'This Caroline tragedy
centres on the relationship between an
idealistic actor (Paris) and his patron, the
power-crazed tyrant, Dominitian Caesar.
The drama is played out in a succession
of theatrical locations; the Swan providing
the perfect arena for senate and palace.
The settings for a series of plays within
plays are created by the actors, with poles
and cloths. Before this ad hoc scenery,
Paris' powerful argument for the value of
drama crumbles as his company's
productions, at best, have no positive
effect on the assembled audience and,
at worst, inspire desire and brutality.
The clothing, props, benches and tower
truck enabled us to move swiftly from
scene to scene and to create our version
of Rome: a beautiful but primitive, dirty and
corroded place where stifled subjects
cower and flies swarm. Death and decay
are never far away.'

Director: Sean Holmes
Set and Costume Designer: Anthony Lamble
Lighting Designer: Wayne Dowdeswell
Photographer: Anthony Lamble

Stefanos Lazaridis

English National Opera
Italian Opera Season

London Coliseum
September - December 2000

Stefanos Lazaridis: 'Eight operas in
13 weeks - all new productions - but on a
budget equivalent to an average season
of three new productions and six revivals.
The grand plan was to deconstruct the
London Coliseum and to celebrate
"flamboyant poverty" within the ruins of a
collapsing theatre. The holding feature of
the auditorium environment allowed us to
represent each opera in a more skeletal
form, behind or within the proscenium.
It also provided performance spaces
within the auditorium itself and the option
to place the orchestra in a variety of
unusual positions on stage, as well as
in the pit.

Manon Lescaut	**The Coronation of Poppea**	**Nabucco**
Giacomo Puccini	*Claudio Monteverdi*	*Giuseppe Verdi,*
Text by Praga, Oliva and Illica after Prévost	*Text by Giovanni Francesco Busenello*	*Text by Temistocle Solera*
September 2000	*September 2000*	*November 2000*
Director: Keith Warner	*Director: Steven Pimlott*	*Director: David Pountney*
Set and Costume Designer: Stefanos Lazaridis	*Set Designer: Stefanos Lazaridis*	*Assistant Set Designer and Model Maker:*
Assistant Set Designer and Model Maker:	*Assistant Set Designer and Model Maker:*	*Matthew Deeley*
Matthew Deeley	*Matthew Deeley*	*Set Designer: Stefanos Lazaridis*
Associate Costume Designer: Emma Ryott	*Costume Designer: Ingeborg Berneth*	*Costume Designer: Marie-Jeanne Lecca*
Lighting Designer: Davy Cunningham	*Lighting Designer: Peter Mumford*	*Lighting Designer: Davy Cunningham*
Choreographer: Yolande Snaith	*Choreographer: Jonathan Lunn*	*Photographer (model): Vassilis Skopelitis*
Environment Consultant: Peter Ruthven Hall	*Photographer (model): Vassilis Skopelitis*	
Photographer (model): Vassilis Skopelitis		

Sophie Jump

Removed

Seven Sisters Group
London Contemporary Dance School Library
London
February 2001

Sophie Jump: 'We tried to create an atmosphere in which it was as though the character inhabited the space of the library and was constantly absorbing and regurgitating sections of text, words and letters. We rehearsed almost exclusively in the space and worked very closely together as a team, creating images, spoken pieces and movement together. The audience walked through the space and were in very close proximity to the dancer, able to see small letters on her tongue or read the words written all over her body.'

Choreographer: Susanne Thomas
Set and Costume Designer: Sophie Jump
Lighting Designer: Simon Corder
Dancer: Claire Burrell
Composer: Phil Durrant
Photographer: Mattias Ek

Pamela Howard

La Celestina
Fernando de Rojas. Adapted by Pamela Howard and Robert Potter

Dartmouth College at Hoskins Center Hanover, New Hampshire, USA February 2002

The traverse stage
Scene 1 The first 'Paseo'

Pamela Howard: 'The auditorium is changed. Blue sheets are draped over the seats, with little boats accented in a rippling light to represent the sea. The audience is directed to walk on to the stage through two proscenium doors to discover another auditorium. Walls and staging are painted terracotta, in large bold brushstrokes and represent a town by the sea. The traverse stage is a street, 17.5m x 1.8m, with a raked platform at each end. The audience sits facing the street and is then directed by light, sound and movement to turn and watch the scenes at either end. This makes the production move swiftly as the play progresses, without scene changes, from comedy in Scene 1 to tragedy in Scene 16. The audience is excited and expectant, finding itself in this unusual new space so close to the actors.'

Director: Pamela Howard
Set Designers:
Pamela Howard
with Georgi Alexi Meskhishvili
Costume Designers:
Pamela Howard
with Margaret Spicer
Lighting Designer: Dan Kotlowitz
Choreographer:
Ronni Stewart-Laughton
Composer: John Sheldon
Photographer: John Sheldon

Levitt Bernstein Associates

Stratford Circus
Performing Arts Centre

Stratford, East London
June 2001

Gary Tidmarsh: 'It is not easy to design a good performance space for small to medium -scale drama. It is even more difficult when the self-same theatre must also transform itself into a venue for dance, literature, comedy, cabaret and music of all kinds. In our recent design for the new performing arts centre at Stratford Circus, dance and drama are the major features of the mixed programme in an auditorium that has adaptable stage, seating and shape. Working with the end-users, the design was explained then evolved using multi-media, sketches, models and computer animation.'

Client: London Borough of Newham
Architect: Levitt Bernstein Associates
Theatre Consultant: Theatre Projects
Structural Engineer: Whitby Bird
Services Engineers: Battle McCartney
Photographer: Morley von Sternberg

Fred Meller

Ghost Ward
Devised by the company

Almeida Theatre Company
A disused derelict Hospital in Bow - London
May 2001

Fred Meller: 'A site-specific production begins with a bus journey to a disused hospital. How would contemporary theatre respond to the paradoxical nature of a space that we would want to leave as soon as we arrived? In this site, reality of "the living" is reinforced by 2D images: get well cards, photos of home and family, books, paintings. Photographs of past patients create a "wall of fame". In my design the 2D image becomes a performative, a memento, a theatrical text and is loaded and dynamic. Enlarged X-ray lightboxes which support images describe, punctuate and question the controversial exploration of life poised on possible death. 2D to 3D; 3D to 2D - There and back.'

Director: Ben Harrison
Set Designer: Fred Meller
Lighting Designer: Natasha Chivers
Composer: Philip Pinsky

Rosemarie Cockayne

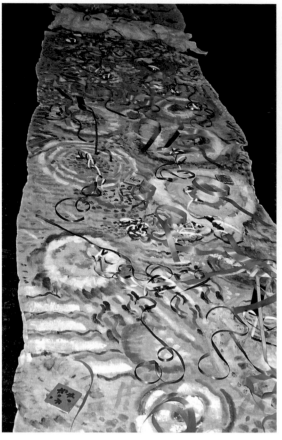 

River of Life
Devised

*Unleash and St Martin's-in-the-Fields Social
Care Unit
St Martin's-in-the-Fields - London
November 2000*

Rosemarie Cockayne: 'Many people die
homeless in London each year. This was an
installation for a service of remembrance
for friends, carers and the public. The river
flowed from three boulders, with a single
shell, around the altar. Canvas and net
were painted in patterns representing fish,
grass, shells, stones and enamelled tiles,
created with users of the shelters. As the
congregation entered, they received a
ribbon. During the service, they were
invited to place their ribbon with a prayer
of the heart, into the river. As the names of
those who had died were read out,
everyone went forward to light a candle.'

*Directors: Pat Logan, Rev. Janet Woolton, Rev.
Rosemary Lain-Priestley, Roger Shalgean
Set and Costume Designer:
Rosemarie Cockayne
Music: St Martin's-in-the-Fields Social
Care Unit Group, Academy of St Martin's-in-
the-Fields, Annabel Clark, John Deacon
Photographer: Rev. Rosemary Lain-Priestley*

Simon Corder

Postcard from Morocco
*John Donahue and
Dominick Argento*

*Guildhall School
of Music and Drama
London - June 2002*

'The scene is like memory, like an old postcard
from a foreign land showing the railway station
of Morocco or some place, hot and strange.'
(John Donahue)

Simon Corder: 'We used a length of
railway, steel and concrete, as a catwalk
extending from a cabaret stage.
The audience and singers sat at tables.
The track introduced a delicious tension to
the evening and was a fine object to bring
into the theatre space. The setting was
computer modelled. There was no
traditional model box.'

*Director: Martin Lloyd Evans
Set Designer: Simon Corder
Costume Designer: Frank Simon
Lighting Designer: Simon Corder
Choreographer: Isabel Mortimer
Conductor: Michael Fulcher*

Gabriella Csanyi-Wills

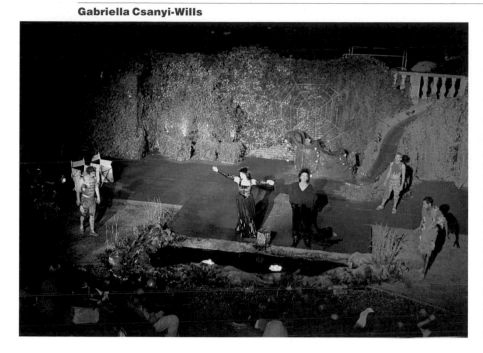

A Midsummer Night's Dream
William Shakespeare

Attic Theatre Company
Cannizaro Park - London
August 1999

Gabriella Csanyi-Wills: 'Cannizaro Park needed little to emphasise the grand gardens of the Duke or the magical world of the fairies: a slide, a pond (in which Hermia and Helena fought), a bower (a large, trucked oval bed), moving trees and a gigantic spider's web, all partially or fully covered with foliage. The costumes were given a period feel, but nothing too specific. The fabrics directly or indirectly reflected the colours of the park: Titania and Oberon, with an Acer tree; the fairies, with an ivycovered brick wall, confusing the "illusory with the real" (Stanley Wells) and a "merrier hour (or two) was never wasted there (Puck)."

Director: Jenny Lee
Set and Costume Designer:
Gabriella Csanyi-Wills
Lighting Designer: Mike King
Choreographer: Geoffrey Unkovitch
Sound and Music: Paul Todd
Photographer: Dave Smith

Soutra Gilmour

Tear from a Glass Eye
Matt Cameron

Gate Theatre Company
The Gate Theatre
London
February 2000

Soutra Gilmour: 'The design process was mostly concerned with responding to the structure of the text. The scenes journey from one place to another, sometimes forward, sometimes folding back on themselves: a modern Australian walkabout. Taking a line for a walk through the space of the Gate gave it the possibility of dimensions determined by the architectural features and audience landscape. In turn this allowed it to become the places of the play: runway, beach, hangar, desert crossroads and crashed aircraft.'

Director: Erica Whyman
Set and Costume Designer: Soutra Gilmour
Lighting Designer: Malcolm Rippeth

Scale Project

New Town
Scale Project

Harlow Town Hall and Civic Square
December 2001

Arches Theatre - Glasgow
April 2002

Paul Burgess and Simon Daw: '*New Town* is a series of collaborations using site-specific and theatre locations to create a performance in which real and imaginary architectural worlds blur, as the characters struggle with the responsibility of designing a new town. The audience finds its own route through multi-layered narratives and the complex spaces of an installation environment that is both planning office and planned city. Changing the combination of overlapping sections and moments of improvisation we created a continually evolving structure.'

Set Designers: Paul Burgess and Simon Daw
Lighting Designer:
Katharine Williams (Harlow)
Scale Project (Glasgow)
Video: James Lapsley
and Scale Project (Glasgow)
Sound: Andrew Flett (Glasgow)

Simon Wilkinson

Lion in the Streets
Judith Thompson

Arches Theatre - Glasgow
May 2001

Simon Wilkinson: '*Lion in the Streets* follows the central character's journey through a surreal, suburban landscape, from a desolate playground, past increasingly disturbing scenes, sharing her realisation of her death and the confrontation with her murderer.
The concept of this journey was central to the production. When logistical constraints reduced the physical journey to the distance between two converted railway arches, lighting came to the fore. The play opens and concludes in one empty arch, with the central action taking place in a seated space in the other. With a limited budget, the definition of different spaces became dependent on lighting, resulting in an intensive, collaborative process between director, designer and lighting designer.'

Director: Adrian Osmond
Set and Costume Designer: Brian Hartley
Lighting Designer: Simon Wilkinson
Photographer: Brian Hartley

Alan Schofield

The Novello Theatre

Sunninghill, Ascot
1999-2002

Alan Schofield: 'Reality and fantasy mingle at the Novello Theatre. This is a rare, building-based company performing for children. Like Topsy, this project just grew. A false proscenium, painted as a 19th-century toy theatre, was used as part of the scenic design for a pantomime. It remained for the next production and the next. Soon, the design spread along the walls of the theatre. From painted boxes, 2D characters from the Novello's productions join the audience of real, 3D children. Through *trompe l'oeil* painting, the squareness of the converted, burnt-out cinema has been given added shape with fashionable round-ended boxes of the 1820s.'

Designer and Scenic Artist: Alan Schofield

Cathy Ryan

Millennium Mysteries

Belgrade Theatre with Teatr Biuro Podrozy
Coventry Cathedral Ruins
July 2000

Above: Noah's Ark and Flood Angels
Above right: Adam and Eve on the Tree of Life

Cathy Ryan: 'Millennium Mysteries was enacted in the dramatic setting of the floodlit ruins of Coventry Cathedral. Designing costumes for the Old Testament involved close collaboration with the set designer and three directors, each dealing with a different part of the Bible.

A contemporary and visual approach, with minimal script, enabled the large cast of local people to explore the epic themes of Genesis, the Flood, and Exodus, using movement, spectacle, and music.
In Genesis, Adam and Eve were played by two intrepid pensioners on swings, hung from the huge, metal Tree of Life, which burst into flames at the wrath of God. Their costumes were influenced by the medieval pagan concepts of the Green Man and the Goddess. In the Flood, Noah was played by a Rastafarian, the costumes for his family based upon woven, African textiles and linens.

Directors: Richard Hayhow,
Kathi Leahy and Janet Steel
Set Design: Tom Conroy
Costume Design: Cathy Ryan
Lighting Designer: Bernie Howe
Photographer: Ian Tilton

The production was nominated for a Barclay's/TMA award for Best Design

Keith Williams Architects

Unicorn Theatre for Children

Tooley Street - London
Completion date: 2005 check

Keith Williams: 'My designs for the new building have been influenced by Tony Graham's ground-breaking theatrical work, but also derive from a deep understanding of the building programme, the building's context, and the Unicorn's commitment to be fully accessible for children. The new building will provide a 350-seat theatre, a theatre studio, education, teaching and rehearsal spaces, and will be the most far-reaching child focused educative and theatrical cultural institution in the UK. The larger architectural gestures of spectacularly projecting main auditorium and the iconic corner tower, with its eroded base, signal the new building at an urban level, yet the designs are also rich in child-scale detail. Stages, balconies, seating and in particular the form of the main auditorium itself derived from narrative storytelling, all bring a delicate and appropriate scale to a unique new theatre for children.'

Architects: Keith Williams Architects
Theatre Consultants: Theatre Projects Consultants
Artistic Director (Theatre): Tony Graham
Photographer: Eamon O'Mahony

Louise Ann Wilson

Mapping the Edge
*Amanda Dalton, Bernardine Evaristo and Alison Fell.
Music by Kuljit Bhamra*

*Wilson&Wilson Company and Crucible Theatre Co-Production
Site-specific – Sheffield
September 2001*

Louise Ann Wilson: 'Mapping the Edge is a site-specific production inspired by the city of Sheffield and the ancient Greek myth of Medea. This multi-site performance took its audience of 33 people on a journey by bus, tram and on foot, to familiar landmarks and forgotten places. These included a buried urban garden, a disused cutlery works, a boxing ring and the underground City Hall Ballroom. Three interweaving stories unfolded seamlessly around them at the sites and during the journey itself.
The living landscape of the city became the stage as the frontier between drama and reality was challenged.'

*Created and directed by:
Wils Wilson
Created and designed by:
Louise Ann Wilson
Lighting designed by:
Natasha Chivers
Photographer: Dominic Ibbotson*

Ian Teague

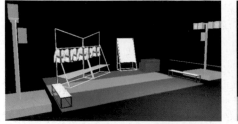
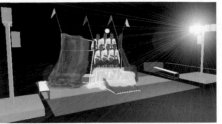
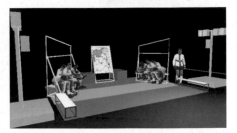

Henry V
William Shakespeare
Adapted by Daniel Buckroyd

Education Department
Nuffield Theatre - Southampton
Touring schools and arts centres
November 2001

Ian Teague: 'In the past four years I have used an increasing amount of IT in my design process. These three images are from a storyboard created entirely on computer. This football-themed *Henry V* used a few simple, movable metal structures to create locations ranging from a changing room to the siege of Harfleur. I created (alongside a physical model) a 3D computer model, using Truespace, with which I worked out how each scene would work. I then generated rendered views of each scene, which I exported to Paintshop Pro. In this 2D programme I added more detail to create the storyboard.'

Director: Mathew Cullem
Set and Costume Designer: Ian Teague

Roma Patel

Skeletons of Fish
Keith Antar Mason and Joseph Jones

Hittite Empire (USA) and Chakra Zulu (UK), commissioned and produced by LIFT Studio 2, Riverside Studios - London July 2001

Roma Patel: 'The use of 3D computer modelling for the pre-visualisation of my ideas was the most obvious solution for this project. The challenge was to communicate my design ideas for the set, costumes and projections to theatre practitioners in the USA and the UK. I needed the flexibility to adapt and change the model quickly and to publish it on an internet-based, visual design diary, set up especially for this project and only accessible to the production team. The communication continued via the internet and e-mail until mid May, when the entire company and the production team were brought together in London.'

Directors: Keith Antar Mason and Joseph Jones
Set and Costume Designer: Roma Patel
Lighting Designer: Ian Scott
Choreographer: Keith Antar Mason
Sound Designer: Nick Manning

Costume design

Many of the designers in this section also design sets. Costume design is a separate section under the 2D>3D theme because of the variety of ways in which the idea for a costume becomes a 3D reality in performance.

The emphasis on virtuoso drawing by the designer has given way to acceptance of a wide variety of styles of illustration, notably collage techniques, often incorporating photocopies and digital manipulation of scanned materials and information.[1]

Costume designs may be presented for single characters, or scene by scene, showing all the characters present at any one moment.[2] Sometimes the atmospheric impact of a costume drawing is considered all important[3] although separate line drawings showing details,[4] side and back views are always valuable and often essential.

The costume design drawing is only the beginning of a dialogue between the designer and the maker or costume supervisor. Designers may choose to be present when patterns are cut or may wait to see the prototype or toile on the actor before deciding on the final shape and detail.

The purpose of the 2D design is to hint, through line and texture, at the solidity and completeness of the finished garment. Fabric samples may be selected before the design is completed, where the designer wants to establish 'a look' before the individual details. At other times they will be specially dyed, printed or painted to the specific requirements of the design.[5]

1 Claire Lyth, Twelfth Night p00, Marie-Jeanne Lecca, Turandot p33
2 Kate Burnett, Oklahoma! p25
3 David Collis, Oliver Twist p26
4 Tanya McCallin, Rigoletto p31
5 Peter McKintosh, Alice p34, Emma Ryott, Manon Lescaut p33

Anne Curry

The Tempest
William Shakespeare

*The Birmingham Theatre School,
Crescent Theatre Studio
Birmingham
May 2002*

Anne Curry: 'The Crescent Studio is an
intimate space with the audience seated
on three sides - very close. This triptych of
Ariel shows how she was seen from each
of the three seating areas. My inspiration
for the way she looked came from exotic
birds, American Indians and contemporary
fashion. Additional jewellery was used for
its sound as much as its appearance.

*Director: Paul Clarkson
Set and Costume Designer:
Anne Curry
Lighting Designer: Paul Clarkson
Choreographer: Mandy Ashwood
Music: Pete Hammond*

Cecily Kate Borthwick

Moby Dick
*Jim Burke, adapted from the novel
by Herman Melville*

*Walk the Plank and Kaboodle
The Fitzcarraldo, a former Norwegian ferry,
now a touring theatre
May 2000*

Cecily Kate Borthwick:
The costumes for *Moby Dick* were hand-
painted to create a washed-out, ghostly
appearance. This effect aided the
illustrative look of the production as an epic
sea-faring story, told by Ishmael, its only
survivor. Old-fashioned engravings from
The Rhyme of The Ancient Mariner by
Gustav Doré were projected on to the
upstage cyclorama: storm scenes of
sailors clinging to the rigging; distant ships
on the horizon; and vast ocean vistas
added perspective to the 3D ropes and
rigging of the set.

*Director: Lee Beagley
Set and Costume Designer:
Cecily Kate Borthwick
Lighting Designers: Geoff Farmer
and Patrick Collins
Composer: Andy Frizell
Photographer: Paul Herrmann*

*2001 Manchester Evening News
Award - Best Fringe Production
2001 Manchester Evening News
Award - Best New Play*

Kate Burnett

Oklahoma!
Richard Rodgers and Oscar Hammerstein II

*National Youth Music Theatre
Waterfront Hall - Belfast and touring
August 2002*

Kate Burnett: 'With a cast of 35, expanses of floor for big dance numbers and an opening in a large concert hall (but touring venues unknown), the design needed to be able to adapt to a variety of spaces. The vigorous stripes and checks say something about the bright, clashing life of the American frontier. Conceived as an ensemble piece, my costume drawings were sketch-schemes of groups of characters. I sampled the fabrics before committing to colouring these drawings. The process was a little like creating a patchwork quilt, with colour and pattern references and links made back and forth between the characters and groups of chorus.'

*Director: Roger Haines
Set and Costume Designer: Kate Burnett
Lighting Designer: Nick Richings
Choreographer: Kay Shepherd
Music Director: Jonathan Gill*

David Collis

Oliver Twist
Richard Williams, after Charles Dickens

Liverpool Playhouse
November 2001

David Collis: 'A giant "ski jump" of rotting timbers projected out into the auditorium; perforated with traps and metal rungs, it allowed the actors to teem in all directions. The clothes, all tonally related to the set, added to the sense of *chiaroscuro*, restlessness and menace that pervades the narrative.'

Director: Richard Williams
Set and Costume Designer: David Collis
Lighting Designer: David Horn
Choreographer: Jenny Weston

Celia Perkins

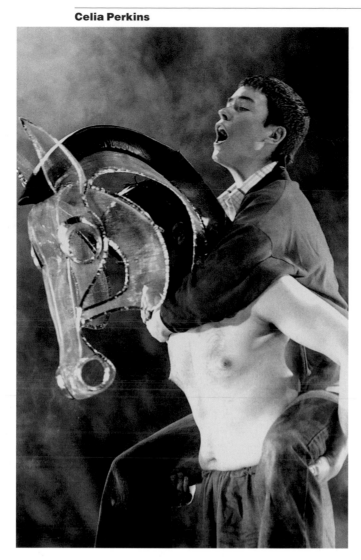

Equus
Peter Shaffer

Oldham Coliseum Theatre
February 2001

Celia Perkins: 'The Equus head was designed as a series of metallic mesh, 2D forms, sculpted into a 3D mask. It enabled the audience to see fully the actor's head working in the space within it, never detracting from the fact that the horse was an actor. For reference, the maker and I looked in detail at Greek and Roman sculpture as well as at medieval and Tudor, equine armour. The image of the actor's flesh against the metal gauze and leather mane gave a naked vulnerability, in contrast to the powerful 3D form recognised when first seeing the "armoured" actor.'

Director: Rod Natkiel
Set and Costume Designer: Celia Perkins
Lighting Designer: Phil Davies
Mask Maker: Julia Walker
Photographer: Joel Fildes

Ann Curtis

The School for Scandal
Richard Brinsley Sheridan

Stratford Festival Company of Canada and Chicago Shakespeare Theater
Stratford Festival Theatre - Stratford, Ontario
August 1999

Ann Curtis: 'Lady Sneerwell, the leader of her fashionable school for scandal, has rushed (always with an eye for drama) to gloat over the delicious possibility of a mortal outcome to a duel, recently fought by two of her intimate acquaintances. But, now caught by malicious tittle-tattle, she is shocked into nearly betraying her secret fancy for the free-spirited young man, whose love affair she is working to destroy.'

Director: Richard Monette
Set and Costume Designer: Ann Curtis
Lighting Designer: Michael J Whitfield
Choreographer: John Broome
Photographer: Avon Studios

Paul Farnsworth

Follies
Book by James Goldman,
music and lyrics by Stephen
Sondheim

Raymond Gubbay and the Royal
Festival Hall - London
August 2002

Paul Farnsworth: 'It is 1971. We are in the
fictional Weismann Theatre on Broadway.
The showgirls who worked here in the
1930s meet once more before the building
is demolished to make way for a car park.
The theatre is haunted by the younger
showgirls dressed in white, silver and grey,
in stark contrast to the bright colours of
contemporary 1971. The costumes are

very large - especially the
head-dresses - to fill the space
of the cavernous stage.'

Director: Paul Kerryson
Set and Costume Designer:
Paul Farnsworth
Lighting Designer: Jenny Cane
Choreographer: David Needham

Paul Edwards

Die Zauberflöte
Wolfgang Amadeus Mozart.
Text by Emanuel Schikaneder

The New Israeli Opera,
Opera House - Tel Aviv
November 1999

Paul Edwards: 'Papageno is a bird
catcher. To emphasise his bird-like
qualities, he is dressed as a decoy.
Papagena, his ideal woman, is
transformed into a flamingo show-girl.'

Director: Michael McCaffery
Set Designer: Michael McCaffery
Costume Designer: Paul Edwards
Lighting Designer: Michael Scott

Becky Hawkins

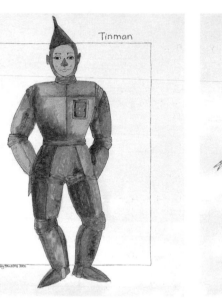

The Wizard of Oz
L Frank Baum

*Northcott Young Company,
Northcott Theatre - Exeter,
April 2000*

Becky Hawkins. 'Naturally, everyone expects *The Wizard of Oz* to look just like the film. So I put a spin on it, making the design my own, while acknowledging the limited budget. Dorothy is a tomboy, feisty and practical, definitely not a girlie girl, and she speaks her mind. The main characters are toys from Dorothy's childhood. As the last things she sees before the cyclone hits, they are incorporated into her dreams. In rehearsals with the large teenage cast, we became very aware of the story as a metaphor for the journey of growing up. The witches symbolise the two poles of adult behaviour (and sexuality). Glinda, the rainbow personified, contrasts with the darkly powerful Wicked Witch of the West. I wanted to get away from pointy hats and stripey socks, and trousers are so much more practical for riding a broomstick!'

*Director: Rachel Vowles and
John Whitehead
Set and Costume Designer:
Becky Hawkins
Lighting Designer: Jon Primrose
Musical Director: Paul McClure*

Claire Lyth

Twelfth Night
William Shakespeare

*National Theatre of Norway – Oslo
February 2002*

*Olivia's costumes
Far left: Cesario between Olivia and Orsino
Below: Olivia on a motorbike*

Claire Lyth: 'Olivia's journey through a modern production of *Twelfth Night*. From veiled mourning she reinvents herself with every scene, in her effort to win Cesario. She later succeeds in driving Cesario/ Sebastian away on a Harley Davidson. Subsequently, the sophisticated poseur gives way to a barefoot romantic - the bike cover donned for a hasty marriage, a white satin sheet for Act V. By creating a body for each scene digitally, it was possible to redesign the costumes as ideas progressed, without starting again each time, finally adding the actress's face.'

*Director: Ragnar Lyth
Set and Costume Designer: Claire Lyth
Lighting Designer: Linus Fellbom
Composer: Åsmund Feidje
Photographer: Morten Krogvold*

Rebecca Hurst

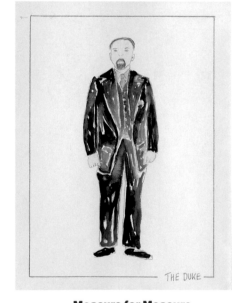
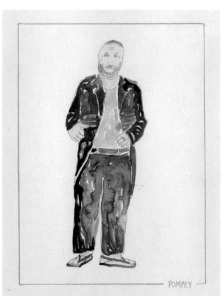

Measure for Measure
William Shakespeare

*Cambridge Arts Theatre
June 2002*

Rebecca Hurst: 'The authoritarian characters of the play wore slick, dark power suits. To counter this I dressed the populace in more edgy, streetwise and occasionally bizarre clothing in a wider palette of colours.'

*Director: Stephen Siddall
Set and Costume Designer: Rebecca Hurst
Lighting Designer: Alistair Boitz*

Tanya McCallin

Rigoletto
Giuseppe Verdi
Text by Francesco Maria Piave after
Victor Hugo

Royal Opera House – London
September 2001

Tanya McCallin: 'Act 1, scene 1: Marullo:-
one of the "beautiful people" at the court of
the Duke of Mantua - early 16th century.
We used literally hundreds of paintings,
frescos and drawings of the French and
Italian Renaissance to make close study of
period detail. Sketches were made to
select, distil and freely interpret information
to suggest the hierarchical world of the
piece. All the clothes were made of
lustrous silks and damasks, in gorgeous
colours, with emphasis placed on points
and lacings to achieve a louche and
debauched look for this, the Ball Scene.'

Director: David McVicar
Set Designer: Michael Vale
Costume Designer: Tanya McCallin
Lighting Designer: Paule Constable
Choreographer: Leah Hausman
Photographer: Clive Barda

Martin Johns

2 MUNCHKIN TEACHERS   "THE" WIZARD OF OZ

The Wizard of Oz
L Frank Baum

Theatre by the Lake - Keswick
December 2002

Martin Johns: 'Having left a monochrome Kansas via a shadow-play "twister", Munchkinland was the first appearance of strong colour in the production. We based the look on the idea of American quilts and gave all the costumes a more heightened padded and patchwork look. All the costumes were backed and appliquéd on to wadding. Because the Munchkins' favourite colour was blue, this became the dominant theme, using soft yellows, pinks and greens to offset it. The set elements also echoed this more rounded and patchwork feel.'

Director: Ian Forrest
Set and Costume Designer: Martin Johns
Lighting Designer: Nick Beadle
Choreographer: Lorelei Lynn

Marie-Jeanne Lecca

Macbeth
Giuseppe Verdi
Text by Francesco Maria Piave after Shakespeare

Opernhaus Zürich - Switzerland
July 2001

Marie-Jeanne Lecca: 'The Macbeths' lack of children and heirs, and the subject of giving birth - whether to a child or a demon - runs throughout the show. It starts with one of the witches, the pregnant one, stroking her tummy with circular movements. It finishes with 25 children appearing as Banquo's heirs and then becoming Birnham Wood. The intensely red world of the witches created a balanced complement to the brutal grey-black scars of war, the army's breastplates suggesting stylised human muscles. Against this landscape, the frail silhouettes of the children, bearers of hope, carry the green sap of life.'

Director: David Pountney
Set Designer: Stefanos Lazaridis
Costume Designer: Marie-Jeanne Lecca
Lighting Designer: Jürgen Hoffmann
Choreographer: Vivienne Newport
Conductor: Franz Welser-Möst

Emma Ryott

Manon Lescaut
Giacomo Puccini
Text by Praga, Oliva and Illica after Prévost

English National Opera, Italian Opera Season
London Coliseum
September 2000

Emma Ryott: 'The costumes reflect a world of decadence and decay. We decided to push Stefanos' original concept of plastered, 18th-century, ghostly figures one stage further by making the chorus resemble birds of prey; voyeuristic parasites observing and feeding off the action below. Feather decoration served to reinforce this idea while cracked, plastered fabric gave the costumes a sinister (un)reality - particularly effective when the performers passed through the auditorium. By contrast we keep the principals' costumes unplastered and in rich colours to separate them from the world of corruption and to underline the emotional intensity of their story.'

Director: Keith Warner
Set and Costume Designer: Stefanos Lazaridis
Associate Costume Designer: Emma Ryott
Lighting Designer: Davy Cunningham
Choreographer: Yolande Snaith
Photographer: Andy Wale

Turandot
Giacomo Puccini
Text by Adami and Simoni after Gozzi

Grosses Festspielhaus - Salzburg
August 2002

Marie-Jeanne Lecca: '*Turandot* is the story of a man-hating princess, transformed by love. She confines herself in a self-mutilating world, a sexless society, inhabited by nasty, puppet-like automata, with dismembered bits of mechanisms attached to their clothes. A Chinese touch was retained in the cut of the jackets and in the masks, where Chinese Opera make-up was given sharper, more angular and aggressive lines.'

Director: David Pountney
Set Designer: Johan Engels
Costume Designer:
Marie-Jeanne Lecca
Costumes made by the
Salzburger Festspiele Workshops
Sculptor mechanical pieces:
Peter Braunreuther
Lighting Designer: Jean Kalman
Choreographer: Beate Vollack
Conductor: Valery Gergiev

Peter McKintosh

Alice in Wonderland and Through the Looking Glass
Adrian Mitchell, adapted from Lewis Carroll

*Royal Shakespeare Company
Barbican Theatre - London
Royal Shakespeare Theatre -
Stratford upon Avon
November 2001*

Peter McKintosh: 'Most people have such strong images of how Alice should look, be it Tenniel, Peak, Disney or Ralph Steadman. My designs retained 2D images in the settings but the costumes and characters were very three dimensional!'

*Director: Rachel Cavanaugh
Set and Costume Designer: Peter McKintosh
Lighting Designer: Chris Davey
Movement: Linda Dobell
Music: Terry Davies and Stephen Warbeck
Photographer: Manuel Harlan*

Jason Durrant Ions

One Dark Night
David Farmer

*Tiebreak Theatre
Touring theatres and schools
February 2002*

Jason Durrant Ions: 'A compilation of fairy tales from around the world told in music, mime, acting and puppetry. Devising during rehearsals, I used dry colour quickly to sketch ideas and resolve problems in discussion with the director. Here an actor has to quickly become Baba Yaga's house on chicken legs before appearing as the witch. The comedy of chicken-feet wellies and knobbly knees turns to surprise when the house is lowered to the floor and the actor jumps out as the witch in a full-length black skirt, white head scarf and bare feet.'

*Director: David Farmer
Set and Costume Designer: Jason Durrant Ions
Lighting Designer: Patrick Nelson*

Nancy Surman

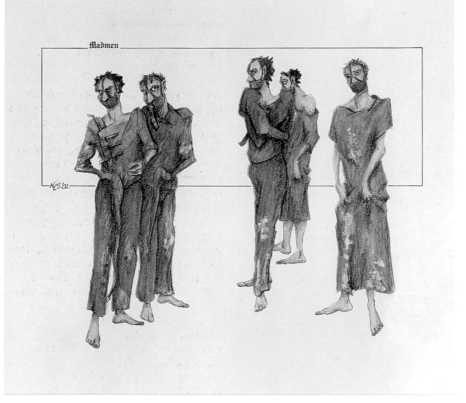

The Duchess of Malfi
John Webster

Salisbury Playhouse
March 2002

Nancy Surman: 'In this classic, Jacobean revenge tragedy, the Duchess of Malfi is ensnared in a rich, powerful, violent, world. Characters spill across the dark, austere landscape like blood, scarlet from a freshly cut vein. The depravity of the Cardinal bestows a hellish corruption on his fiery vestments, while the opulence of the Duchess' sweeping robes shock against the bloody rags of lunatics. The costumes blend Renaissance and contemporary elements. Cut and silhouette are evocative of the period whilst modern fabrics and details, including exotic sari fabrics, give the costumes extraordinary movement, richness and texture.'

Director: Joanna Read
Set and Costume Designer: Nancy Surman
Lighting Designer: Jim Simmons

Madmen

Mayou Trikeriot

Silence and Violence
Torben Betts

Aces and Eights
The White Bear - London
April 2002

Mayou Trikerioti: '*Silence and Violence* is a threateningly timeless play. Fears past and fears future meet in a nameless, suspended present. I tried to make the costumes reflect this ambiguity and by using similar pattern details on different characters in different acts, I let them "echo" each other. That was my way of following the action itself: its violent trans-locations, its unexpected turns and, at the same time, its clasp to its own (un)reality.'

Director: Nick Claxton
Set and Costume Designer: Mayou Trikerioti
Lighting Designer: James Forrester
Assistant Director: Paul Barker
Assistant Designer: Bronia Housman
Head of Wardrobe: Tanya Aanderaa

Abigail Hammond

The Hobbit
JRR Tolkien
Adapted by Glyn Robbins

Vanessa Ford Productions on tour
October 1999

Abigail Hammond: 'As a designer who has worked primarily with dance, the focus is on 2D>3D>movement. In creating the costumes for *The Hobbit*, I sought to enhance and promote a diverse physical approach for each of the inhabitants of Middle Earth. By utilising numerous construction techniques in conjunction with a feast of colour, style, texture and detailing, the visual identities emerged. As the curtain rises for Act 2, the audience gasps when confronted by many people's nightmare - a human-sized arachnid. At the heart of the tale is the struggle of good against evil; at the forefront, sheer fantasy.'

Director: Roy Marsden
Set Designer: David Shields
Costume Designer: Abigail Hammond
Lighting Designer: Robin Carter
Choreographer: Stephanie Carter
Photographer: Catherine Weeks

Sue Willmington

Queen.

Richard II
William Shakespeare

Royal Shakespeare Company
The Other Place - Stratford upon Avon
April 2000
The Pit, Barbican Centre - London
December 2000

Sue Willmington: 'The clothes were
developed during the rehearsal period with
the director and actors. The Queen's
clothes are a way to illustrate her journey
through the play, but her life is otherwise
unclear in the text. Within the season's
"white box" environment, I wanted clear,
crisp shapes that could be timeless.'

Director: Steven Pimlott
Environment Designer: David Fielding
Designer: Sue Willmington
Lighting Designer: Simon Kemp
Composer: Jason Carr

Framing the figure in space

Every set design frames the performer and every costume 'presents' the figure or character it describes. But unlike the subject of a painting, the performer moves and must be at home in any part of the framed space.

The performer in the proscenium picture frame is perceived differently from the performer on a thrust stage or in a theatre in-the-round, where the audience becomes part of the frame. Lighting, scale, colour and proportion are all used to re-contextualise the figure and blend or separate it from its surroundings. [1, 2]

The frame itself is an architectural device and may simply be present in the theatre's own proscenium arch. It may be echoed, distorted or displaced as a device within the design, in order to comment on the artifice of a particular opera or play. Architectural set designs also make use of the framing forms of doorways, windows and balconies. [3]

In some designs, the space around the figure is as much a part of the composition as the shapes made by the performer's body. [4] This is particularly so in dance. [5] In theatre in-the-round, and in open stages, the space between the figures is delineated by the 'landmarks' of furniture, fragments of architectural form and the patterns and textures of floor treatments. Where the audience is looking down, the floor provides one of the most informative elements of any set design. While the vertical frame presents a picture of the performer in the space beyond it, the floor provides a canvas (or prepared ground in painting terms), on which to see the drama or choreography unfold.

1 Es Devlin, God's Plenty p54, Meat p55
2 David Farley, Sexual Perversity in Chicago p47
3 Francis O'Connor, Iphigenia at Aulis p52
4 Alison Chitty, Bacchai p40
5 Anna Fleischle, Babylon p43

Alison Chitty

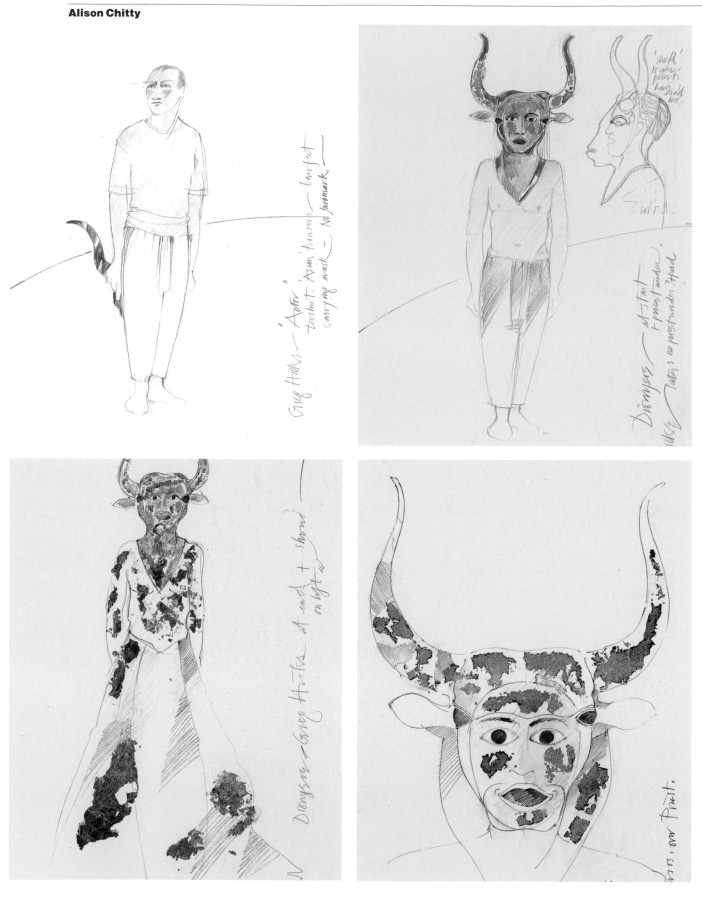

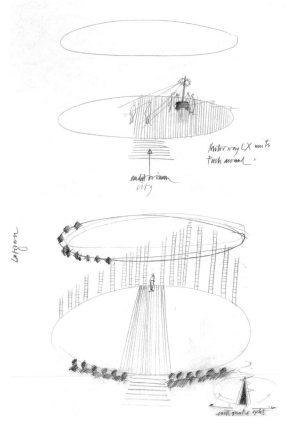

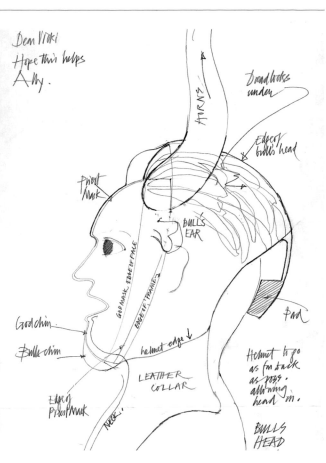

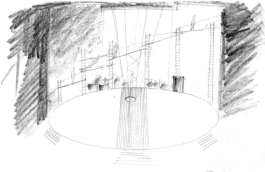

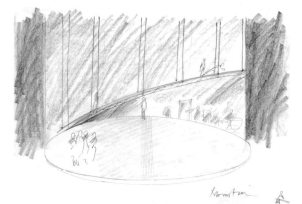

Bacchai

Euripides, in a new version by Colin Teevan

*Olivier Theatre, National Theatre - London
May 2002*

Alison Chitty: 'Two decisions were made before we went into rehearsal for *Bacchai*. Peter Hall was clear he wanted to do the production with masks and that all other decisions would come out of rehearsals. Peter, Harrison Birtwistle, Peter Mumford and I met up to discuss process and we had a one-week workshop at the National Theatre Studio. We worked on ideas with drawings and sketch models, trying to keep up with developments in rehearsal. The production was designed and the music was composed during the nine week rehearsal period; this process was exciting, frightening and sometimes frustrating. We decided on a simple, raked, planked disc with a suspended pathway. Peter Mumford constantly transformed the nature of the space and the action with brilliant shafts of coloured light.'

*Director: Peter Hall
Set and Costume Designer: Alison Chitty
Lighting Designer: Peter Mumford
Composer: Harrison Birtwistle
Sound Designer: Paul Groothuis
Movement Director: Marie-Gabrielle Rotie
Music Directors: Nikola Kodjabashia and Kawai Shiu*

Dody Nash

Animalarky
The Early Earth Operas
John Browne and Jane Buckler

*Commissioned by ENO Baylis.
Performed as part of
St Marylebone Millennium
Mystery Cycle
July 2000*

*They came from the wind
From the wild, wild field
From the desert, from the snow,
From the seabed far below.
Hoof to toe, fin to tail
Every type of creature came
And waited for the rain.*

Dody Nash:'3D preceded 2D in this
celebration of animalkind. I stood in my
studio and choreographed being a giraffe,
a crocodile, a termite... then I physically
imagined adding extensions to parts of my
body to feel more like that animal and drew
what I experienced on to long strips of
paper. When we produced a second
version, in 2001, I taught my design
process to 150 eight-year-olds, who
unhesitatingly came up with 150 further
variations.'

*Director: Steve Moffitt
Set and Costume Designer: Dody Nash*

Kimie Nakano

Sandflower - L'homme blanc
Dance conception: the directors

Korozo Theatre - The Hague
May 2000

Kimie Nakano: ' *L'homme blanc* is sleeping in the oasis. There are twelve balloons - a symbol of hope. He wakes and tries to leave, to discover himself, to be free. When the balloons dry up, he finds freedom. The direction, choreography, set, costumes and music were all involved in creating this meditative space.

Directors: Kimie Nakano
and Megumi Nakamura
Set and Costume Designer: Kimie Nakano
Lighting Designer: Peter Lemmens
Choreographer: Megumi Nakamura

Anna Fleischle

Babylon
Choreography by Olaf Schmidt

National Theatre/Ballet of Baden
Badisches Staatstheater - Karlsruhe
October 1999

Anna Fleischle: 'The idea was to draw a simple but strong shape into the space - versatile and inspiring for the movement within it and malleable through light and movement - to give a feeling of the vast architecture of the crumbling tower of Babylon.'

Choreographer: Olaf Schmidt
Set and Costume Designer: Anna Fleischle
Lighting Designer: Theodor Marquart
Photographer: Günter Krämmer

Tim Skelly

Plunge
Music by Chris Benstead;
Choreography by Janice Garrett

Scottish Dance Theatre, Dundee Rep
September 2000

Tim Skelly: ' The set comprised three gauze screens, so conventional side-lighting was not possible. Low lighting angles from the downstage left and right positions offered fantastic opportunities for shadow play upon the screens, creating a cauldron of moving figures and shadows. This image is of dancers - their identity is as yet undetermined - coming from the shadows towards a trough of light.

Choreographer: Janice Garrett
Set and Costume Designer: Craig Givens
Lighting Designer: Tim Skelly
Photographer: Alan Crumlish

Johanna Town

Les Liaisons Dangereuses
Christopher Hampton,
From the novel by Laclos

Liverpool Playhouse
October 2001

Johanna Town: '*Les Liaisons Dangereuses* is a tour de force of icy elegance, wit and passion played out in Parisian salons and bedrooms. The highly polished, black set was transformed by strong colour washes to create the warmth and opulence of the Paris apartments. Each apartment was symbolised by a different coloured backdrop, which also reflected the mood of the household. The mirror effect of the five-metre box set meant I could use the light's reflection to my advantage, creating dramatic images on the floor and the cyclorama (skycloth) reinforcing a powerful impression of isolation and loneliness between each of the characters.'

Director: Robert Delamere
Set and Costume Designer: Simon Higlett
Lighting Designer: Johanna Town

Andrew Storer

Bach Dances
Johan Sebastian Bach

Dresden Ballet
Semperoper - Dresden
April 2001

Andrew Storer: 'Bach is portrayed as the central figure in a series of dances about inspiration and memory, performed to movements from his Brandenburg and violin concertos. This is one of a series of sketches I made to explore different architectural and spatial contexts for the dance. It was chosen in conjunction with the choreographer to be developed through a model into the final set design. I wanted to imply the classical structure of the music and dance through contemporary imagery and materials.'

Choreographer: Robert North.
Set, Costume and Lighting Designer:
Andrew Storer

Mark Jonathan

Giselle

*Music by Adolphe Adam,
revised by Joseph Horowitz
Choreography by Marius Petipa after Jean
Coralli and Jules Perrot with additional
choreography by David Bintley*

*Birmingham Royal Ballet
Birmingham Hippodrome and touring
September 1999*

Mark Jonathan: 'As midnight sounds, the Wilis-ghosts of young girls who have been jilted before their wedding day avenge themselves by dancing to death any man they happen upon during the hours of darkness. I tried to create an eerie and supernatural quality in the lighting by cross lighting in fine blades of light overlaid with ultra-violet which made the Wilis costumes literally glow in the dark. Dawn breaks, destroying the Wilis' power. Giselle, whose love has transcended death, returns to her grave, but her spirit is finally free. Albrecht is left mourning alone. Very slowly, in the last minutes of the ballet, the first signs of dawn break across the backcloth.
The spirit of Giselle can be seen floating heavenwards above Albrecht.'

*Production: David Bintley and Galina Samsova
Set and Costume Designer: Hayden Griffin
Lighting Designer: Mark Jonathan
Photographer: Bill Cooper*

Christopher Oram

Richard III
William Shakespeare

Crucible Theatre - Sheffield
March 2002

Kenneth Branagh (Richard)
Claire Price (Lady Anne)

Director: Michael Grandage
Set and Costume Designer:
Christopher Oram
Lighting Designer: Tim Mitchell
Photographer: Ivan Kyncl

Christopher Oram: 'Shakespeare wrote his plays for a stage without scenery and only basic drops. So his work is ideally suited to the thrust stage where blocking and sightlines necessitate a simple design solution.'

Plan: Crucible Theatre

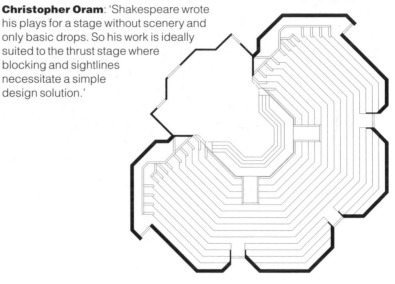

Soutra Gilmour, Bruno Poet

The Birthday Party
Harold Pinter

Crucible Theatre - Sheffield
February 2002

Soutra Gilmour: 'The design challenge of this production was to create the claustrophobic domestic space of the play within the open thrust stage. My solution was to take out the two-dimensional back wall and turn the space into a three-dimensional, in-the-round configuration, finishing the horseshoe auditorium with a fourth bank of seats on stage. This area was occupied only by the solitary figures of Goldberg and McCann watching, then inexplicably entering the house, passing through an invisible wall, while the inhabitants of the house are trapped on a stage, surrounded by the watchful gaze of the audience. Nowhere to escape; nowhere to hide.'

Bruno Poet: 'The audience enter like Goldberg and McCann, mysterious strangers watching and enclosing the domestic space. Naturalism changes to a more filmic style making a surreal atmosphere with strong, soft backlight and then back again to domesticity for Meg's heartbreaking last lines.'

Director: Erica Whyman
Set and Costume Designer: Soutra Gilmour
Lighting Designer: Bruno Poet
Photographer: Ivan Kyncl

Don Juan
Molière. Adapted by Simon Nye

Crucible Theatre - Sheffield
September 2001

Christopher Oram: 'A thrust stage presents one of the ultimate expressions of three-dimensional design. Whereas a proscenium can present the work pictorially - through the "picture frame" - the action on a thrust stage, for two-thirds of the audience, is without the benefit of a backdrop. The floor becomes the key design element and the staging is crucial. Ultimately the most important factor in making the play work is in having a director and actors who understand the space and are confident with the exposing nature of the stage.'

Director: Michael Grandage
Set and Costume Designer: Christopher Oram
Lighting Designer: Hartley T A Kemp
Photographer: Ivan Kyncl

David Farley

The Shawl/
Sexual Perversity in Chicago
David Alan Mamet

Crucible Theatre - Sheffield
November 2001

Director: Angus Jackson
Set and Costume Designer:
David Farley
Lighting Designer: Bruno Poet
Photographer: Ivan Kyncl

David Farley: 'The challenge was to create an intimate environment for the two shows. In *The Shawl*, Mamet reveals little of the story, and this sparse quality needed to be reflected in the design, which was pared down to the bare essentials required by the text. In *Sexual Perversity*, there are 34 scenes, which require a rapid, filmic approach. A small "toolbox" of furniture was designed to facilitate the action, to be moved around and reused for each scene.'

Celia Perkins

Jack and the Beanstalk
Kenneth Alan-Taylor

Oldham Coliseum Theatre
December 2001

Celia Perkins: 'I wanted to design Buttercup as a pantomime cow that was immediately believable as a character in her own right - an animated, 3D object that an audience of screaming five-year-olds and 35-year-olds would want to cuddle and take home. Not wanting to go down saggy fun-fur street, we strove for a more sculptural, rounded form - a hybrid Tweenie/Ermintrude - never losing sight of the all-singing, all-dancing, aah-factor of a pantomime cow!'

Director: Judith Barker
Set and Costume Designer: Celia Perkins
Lighting Designer: Phil Davies
Choreographer: Adele Parry
Prop Maker: Julia Walker

Sue Condie

Sweeney Todd,
the Demon Barber of Fleet Street
Book by Hugh Wheeler
Music and lyrics by Stephen Sondheim

New Vic Theatre - Newcastle under Lyme
May 2002

Sue Condie: '*Sweeney Todd* is set in 1840s London against the backdrop of the Industrial Revolution. This production had to tackle the complexities of a multi-location setting, in-the-round, accommodating a cast of nine, a band and a large chorus playing a variety of other characters. Plenty of quick costume changes saw the stage filled with many different Victorian folk and tradesmen of all classes and those unlucky enough to encounter the fateful blade of Sweeney Todd's razor.'

Director: Chris Monks
Set and Costume Designer: Sue Condie
Lighting Designer: Jo Dawson
Choreographer: Bev Edmunds
Musical Director: Bruce O'Neil

Martin Morley

"Amadeus" First sketch

Amadeus
Peter Shaffer

Cwmni Theatr Gwynedd - Wales
November 2002

Martin Morley: 'The initial sketch was an immediate response to the text and not a design as such. It was useful as a talking point with the director. The design grew from this through a series of doodles and models; the dreams merging with the reality of the modest budget, to create a lavish, opulent environment with simple means where much more was implied than actually stated.'

Director: Graham Laker
Designer: Martin Morley
Lighting Designer: Tony Bailey Hughes

Keith Orton

PROLOGUE

ANTHONY AND TODD ARRIVE IN LONDON

Sweeney Todd, the Demon Barber of Fleet Street
Book by Hugh Wheeler
Music and lyrics by Stephen Sondheim

Central School of Speech and Drama
Embassy Theatre - London
April 2002

Keith Orton: 'The director was keen that the audience would be able to see inside Sweeney Todd's mind. This non-naturalistic approach was enhanced by the nature of the space itself. A stage floor with six traps gave us the opportunity to have characters suddenly appear and disappear. Combining this with three large trucks and three flying flats enabled us to move Sweeney's surroundings both with and against his emotions; sometimes crowding in, at other times leaving him isolated. The storyboarding process enabled both the production team and the cast to buy into the concept.'

Far left: Tobias opens the telling of Sweeney Todd as the company gathers. On the 'whistle' he cranks open a capstan / valve that releases Todd, who rises on a grave trap to the stage.

Left: As the story begins, a back flying piece is removed and towers move towards centre stage. On his entry music, Anthony swings on a ladder hinged to the back of the tower. A 'beggar woman' crawls out of the trap.

Director: John Abulafia
Set Designer: Keith Orton
Costume Designer:
Jessica Bowles
Lighting Designer: Mike Seignior
Sound Designer: Ross Brown
Choreographer: Vanessa Gwan
Musical Director; Wendy Gadian

Kimie Nakano

Yabu No Naka (In the Grove)
Ryunosuke Akutagawa

Cocoon Theatre - Tokyo, Japan
October 1999

Kimie Nakano: 'The first challenge was to play in a new space with a set, rather than a traditional noh kyogen stage. The set had two panels with doors. The play starts in the empty theatre space and finishes in the Tokyo city street. The two panels transform the setting to bamboo groves, a traditional garden, a prison, a temple and a modern city street and a galvanised iron sheet house. The directing, movement and characters were all involved in creating this new modern-traditional theatre space.'

This production won the Award in Art, Japan Festival 1999

Director: Mansai Nomura
Set Designer: Kimie Nakano
Lighting Designer: Kim Yonsu
Photographer: Naoki Hashimoto

David Burrows

A Summer's Day
Slawomir Mrozek

Contemporary Stage Company
The Old Red Lion - London
March 2000

David Burrows: 'As the theatre is so small (so claustrophobic on a first visit, with its completely black floor, walls and ceiling) and as the play's implied locations are exteriors - the park and the beach - I concentrated on suggesting an expansive acting area by using a raised wall of mirror. A slightly elevated floor of laminated light oak planking was surrounded by a similarly toned border of carpet, intended principally for the lady's entrance - gliding silently, in a dappled green light, around the two transfixed men. I generated the artwork for the park scene's background in Photoshop then it was beautifully painted full scale by hand.'

Director: David Graham-Young
Set, Costume and Lighting Designer: David Burrows
Scenic Artist: Faga Cooper-Keeble

Yannis Thavoris

The Rape of Lucretia
Benjamin Britten,
text by Ronald Duncan
after André Obey

English National Opera
Snape Maltings Concert Hall
Aldeburgh
July 2000

Yannis Thavoris: 'A brutalistic portal of oxidised bronze frames everything and echoes the General's decaying armour. The intimacy of the chamber opera expands into a vast, horizontally charged space, where objects, water, fire and human passions resonate with intensity. A mirror extends the space, voyeuristically duplicating the vision of the sleeping Lucretia and the nightmare of her rape.'

Director: David McVicar
Set and Costume Designer:
Yannis Thavoris
Lighting Designer:
Paule Constable

Anna Fleischle

The Mousetrap
Agatha Christie

*Angels Theatre and Film Production
Il Palchetto Stage - Milan
November 2000*

Anna Fleischle: 'The design was a play on the journey from the two-dimensional to the three-dimensional: a flat shape coming to life and becoming three-dimensional, through lighting, movement and the placement of the characters.'

*Director: Matthew Dunster
Set and Costume Designer: Anna Fleischle
Lighting Designer: Drew Pautz
Choreographer: Jane Mason*

Francis O'Connor

Iphigenia at Aulis
*Euripides
Translated by Don Taylor*

*Abbey Theatre - Dublin
March 2001*

Francis O'Connor: 'We wanted to create a space where the sense of off-stage place was as important as the on-stage space: a large hall, perhaps a former temple or public building, is Agamemnon's HQ. Through the upstage doors a poppy field is revealed; interior rooms are unseen stage right and an exterior stage left. The action was updated to the 1940s. On Iphigenia's sacrifice, the wind threw open the huge doors; fans created a blast of air through the space; characters sheltered behind pillars. The moment was both moving and frightening - the wind allowing Agamemnon's fleet to sail to war.'

*Director: Katie Mitchell
Set and Costume Designer: Francis O'Connor
Lighting Designer: Peter Mumford
Photographer: Pat Redmon*

Isabella Bywater

Don Pasquale
Gaetano Donizetti
Text by Giovanni Ruffini and Donizetti

Maggio Musicale Fiorentino
Teatro Communale - Florence
September 2001

Isabella Bywater: 'We set this production in a 17th – 18th-century doll's house. The whole opera takes place in Don Pasquale's house, apart from the final scene, which is outside in the dark, where the duplicity of Norina is revealed and Pasquale realises he has been a fool. The opera was written in 1843 and the costumes of the "dolls" cover periods from the 17th century to the 1830s.'

Director: Jonathan Miller
Set and Costume Designer:
Isabella Bywater
Lighting Designer: Jvan Morandi
Photography: Luca Moggi

Es Devlin

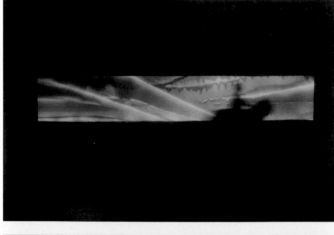

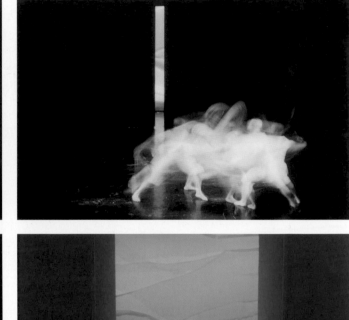

God's Plenty
Music by Dominic Muldowney

Rambert Dance Company
Sadler's Wells Theatre - London
November 1999

Six two-minute moments within the two-hour ballet

Es Devlin: 'The characters in Chaucer's *Canterbury Tales* inhabit a blind foreground with squeezed and stretched blocks beyond; a sculptural landscape framed and re-framed; a dark medieval church with ever mutating windows. The proscenium became the 25th dancer, but with less rehearsal time.'

Choreographer: Christopher Bruce
Set and Costume Designer: Es Devlin
Lighting Designer: Ben Ormerod

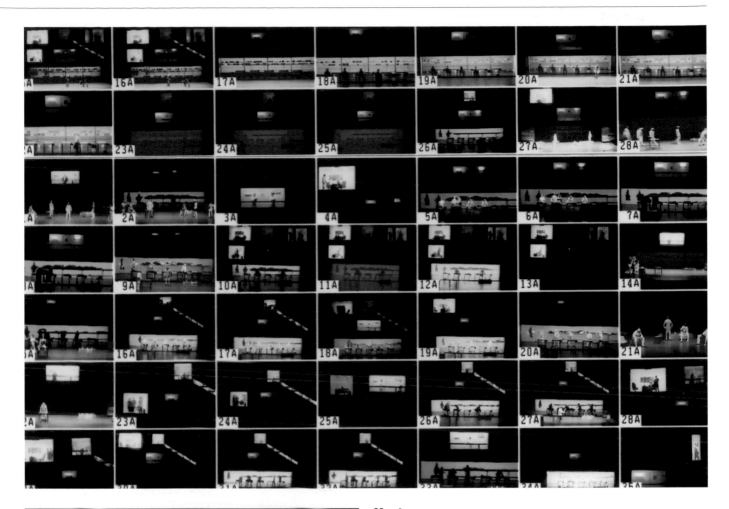

Meat
John O Davies

Theatre Royal - Plymouth
November 2000

Index print showing the use of the compartmentalised proscenium throughout the course of the show.

Es Devlin: 'Manager's office at the top, boning hall at the bottom - the hierarchy of the meat factory. The whistle-blowing foreman caught in the centre. Vets and managers occupy claustrophobic compartments within the proscenium. Only the energy of the boning hall breaks through on to the thrust, accessing the full height of the theatre. Areas could operate simultaneously or in isolation to focus the action into single frames.'

Director: Gemma Bodinetz
Set and Costume Designer: Es Devlin
Lighting Designer: Adam Silverman

Ralph Koltai

Genoveva
Robert Schumann
After Ludwig Tieck and Friedrich Hebbel

Opera North
King's Theatre - Edinburgh
August 2000

Ralph Koltai: 'Genoveva, imprisoned and falsely accused of infidelity, has a vision of freedom.'

Director: David Pountney
Set Designer: Ralph Koltai
Costume Designer: Sue Willmington
Lighting Designer: Paul Pyant
Conductor: Steven Sloane

Kate Burnett

Beauty and the Beast
Charles Way

Library Theatre - Manchester
November 2001

Kate Burnett: 'Dance and movement are written into a script which mixes dreams and reality. A "chamber" set was agreed early in discussions. The walls were largely made up of doors and panels which could open and revolve. This space could be constantly invaded by the "outside" in the form of starry nights, shadowy figures speeding through half open panels, and leaves of the forest creepers climbing up and over the the walls. The bleached-out, beige and gold walls and leaves were designed to be constantly re-coloured and patterned; to appear solid and then to recede with the use of haze and lighting. While storyboarding the play to resolve scene changes and to 'frame' key moments in the story, I realised my main problem - getting a bed on and off stage - could actually be the key. A bed is central to this story of dreams and rites of passage, but only if it could be spun around, transformed, ridden and climbed by all the cast at once! Constantly drawing whilst in dialogue with the director, choreographer, composer and lighting designer, was my way of capturing 3D possibilities in a 2D holding form for long enough to question them and turn them inside out, before committing myself to the actual solution in the model and technical drawings.'

Director: Roger Haines
Set and Costume Designer:
Kate Burnett
Lighting Designer: Nick Richings
Choreographer: Liam Steel
Composer: Richard Taylor

Liz Ascroft

Afterplay
Brian Friel

Gate Theatre - Dublin
March 2002

Liz Ascroft: 'Brian Friel took Sonya from Uncle Vanya and Andrey from The Three Sisters, travelled 20 years forwards and had them meet. We glimpse two whole lives in one sitting. Early on I found a visual opener in the scribble (laid over) of a family tree which I translated into the basic café table layout, with family - separated dead from alive - by the café wall. This layout signals the presence of family as well as desires in this heady and intoxicating atmosphere. Sonya and Andrey become tantalisingly close to each other while exchanging the most important events of their lives that happened outside this room. The closeness of family and unrealised dreams showed themselves as empty tables that only added to the "tundra of aloneness".

Director: Robin Lefevre
Set and Costume Designer: Liz Ascroft
Lighting Designer: Mick Hughes

Keith Dunne

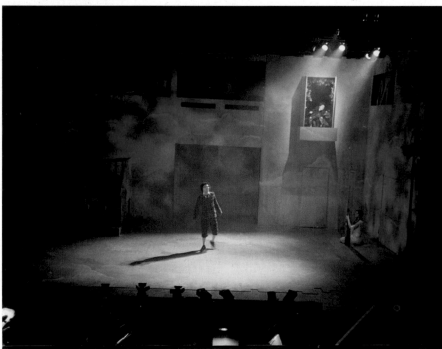

Pinocchio
Devised by the company

Chicken Shed Theatre - London
December 2001

Keith Dunne: 'Chicken Shed Theatre Company focuses on the performers and what they can bring to the performance. In this production I set about designing a flexible world of carpentry and dreams with hidden doors and windows, floorboards, clouds and props. By exploring the full extent of the space and the performers' abilities, we created the extraordinary adventures of Pinocchio at the fastest pace. With scores of children of all ages travelling through this exciting world, it was always good to have those quiet moments when Pinocchio and Geppetto could reflect on the very survival of humanity through bravery, truth, unselfishness and the power to love.'

Director: Mary Ward
Set Designer: Keith Dunne
Costume Designer: Graham Hollick
Lighting Designer: Paul Knowles
Choreographer: Christine Niering
Musical Directors: Jo Collins and David Carey

The line in space

What happens to the 2D line on paper, when it is lifted off the page into three dimensions? This section illustrates designers' fascination with partial, skeletal and suggested forms in which the line retains its integrity, without being 'filled in'.

Sometimes the line structure alludes to a period or style, without applying it wholesale, in a way that might conflict with the more eclectic borrowings of contemporary design. As lines in space, performers can pass between them and be seen beyond them.[1] The forms they describe will only ever be partial, only ever indicating the possibility of a complete building, or the ruin of one.[2]

These 'indications' leave room for the imagination of the viewer to create as much of the image or moment as they require. But the line structure in space can also be immensely strong, working as silhouette;[3] lit to create shadows; framing the figure and creating resonant and dynamic proportions.[4]

The skeletal structure owes some of its popularity to the increased use of steel in scenic building and architecture. Less reinforcement is required and unsupported curves and spans are simpler to create. Computerised cutting of fine lines and details of complex joints have all advanced the possibilities of the streamlined, minimal structure.

There is a debt here to sculptors Julio Gonzalez, who taught Picasso metalwork, and to David Smith who pushed his understanding of Gonzalez' abstract work into creating a large body of drawing and sculpture that explored the space within and beyond the line as something actual and positive, rather than as the negative of the defining line.

1 Madeleine Millar, Doctor Faustus p65
2 Ken Harrison, Passport to Pimlico p62
3 Fiona Watt, The Trestle at Pope Lick Creek p68
4 Michael Pavelka, Henry V p66

Sean Crowley

James and the Giant Peach
Roald Dahl, adapted by David Woods

Sherman Theatre - Cardiff
November 2001

Sean Crowley: 'This version begins in New York, with James and the insects recounting the story. The suggestion of a Manhattan skyline combined with steel frameworks and levels, set on polar revolves, created the movement of the city and the multiple locations required for the story. Revealing the Peach became the significant challenge within the design.'

Director: Phil Clark
Set and Costume Designer: Sean Crowley
Lighting Designer: Ceri James
Musical Director: Paula Gardiner

Bryan Williams

Oklahoma!
Richard Rodgers and Oscar Hammerstein II

Northern Theatre Company
New Theatre - Hull
November 2001

Bryan Williams: 'The design created wide-open space through skeletal, framed structures. The only time the openness was restricted was in the smokehouse scene. Here the roof was lowered, almost to floor level, creating a claustrophobic space. The lighting had to be creatively handled to allow this minimalist set to take on the necessary epic proportions.'

Director: Richard F Green
Set, Costume and Lighting Designer:
Bryan Williams
Choreographer: Julie Burton
Photographer: Bill Ayton

Elroy Ashmore

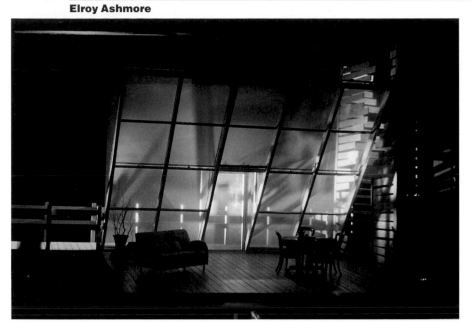

Ghosts
Henrik Ibsen

Haymarket Theatre - Basingstoke
April 2002

Act 2

Elroy Ashmore: 'In this production we stripped away all the heavy Victorian mustiness setting it in the 1950s; still a time of sexual hypocrisy. This is the clear, clean Scandinavian sun room with its sloping glass wall on to which rain fell in Act 1 and hazy, half-seen, ghostly images could be projected. The glazed wall shows transparency: an area where truths must be told. Against this is the older part of the house with its rotten decaying boarding: a place of lies and deceit, all falling apart. The sun room is connected to the outside world by a bridge which perhaps echoes the bridge in Munch's The Scream. At the end everything was dissolved in light.'

Director: Alasdair Ramsay
Set and Costume Designer: Elroy Ashmore
Lighting Designer: David Lawrence

Shakers
John Godber and Jane Thornton

Royal Theatre - Northampton
March 1999

Elroy Ashmore: '*Shakers* is set in a trendy cocktail bar full of life and movement. Just four actors play the waitresses and all their customers that evening. I wanted to give the design the look of cheap neon lights, echoed by primary colours and chrome. All this can be so full of promise and yet, when switched off at the end of the evening, all we are left with is a dirty alley full of fast food rubbish. It's all an illusion. The set was constructed from curved steel and sheet mesh against graffiti-covered brick walls. Curved shapes suggest movement; people on the go, serving food and drinks non-stop.'

Director: Michael Vivian
Set and Costume Designer: Elroy Ashmore
Lighting Designer: Paul Dennant
Choreographer: Stephen Mear

Alex Eales

Tractor Girls
David Holman

Oxfordshire Touring Theatre Company
Touring
January 2002

Alex Eales: 'The set was based on Stalinist architecture: a large, grey box covered in western advertising. The design crosses post-Cold War Russia with the gaudy face of early 21st-century capitalism; a vision of a failing country in economic ruin, running on corruption, bribery and Mafia killings. Two female football fans from Ipswich enter Moscow to see the away leg of their team's long-awaited return to European football. What ensues - loosely described as black comedy - veers from farce to torture. The set transformed as quickly as the action; the folding gauze panels allowing solid walls to become transparent. We move from Moscow airport to a third rate hotel room, ending up in the customs hall at Stansted airport.'

Director: Jeremy James
Set and Costume Designer: Alex Eales
Lighting Designer: Richard G Jones
Photographer: Richard G Jones

Ken Harrison

Passport to Pimlico
T E B Clark
Adapted by Giles Croft

Mercury Theatre - Colchester
February 2000

Ken Harrison: 'In this fable of wish fulfilment, the residents of Pimlico experience a euphoric release from post-war austerity. A framework set serves for various locations above and below ground. In this early scene, a Whitehall official surveys the fishmonger's shop.'

Director: Richard Baron
Set and Costume Designer: Ken Harrison
Lighting Designer: Mark Pritchard

Minty Donald

A Little Rain
Peter Arnott

7:84 Theatre Company
Touring
October 2000

Minty Donald: 'A Glasgow pub in the first year of the new Scottish Parliament – no frills drinking den or slick minimalist symbol of the re-styled city? Either way, it's an inhospitable refuge from the Biblical deluge outside. Not a place to relax - but one in which to drown your sorrows, rake over your roots and maybe pick a fight. Conversation cuts from table to table, from bar to toilet. Fleeting connections spark and fade. Can anything be resolved in this stark, solitary debating chamber?'

Director: Gordon Laird
Set and Costume Designer: Minty Donald
Lighting Designer: Dave Shea
Composer: David Young
3D Computer Model: Minty Donald

Roger Maidment

Moll Flanders
Claire Luckham
Based on a novel by Daniel Defoe

Steel Wasp Theatre Company
Touring
September 2001

Roger Maidment: '*Moll Flanders* is a rambling 18th-century novel. Claire Luckham's adaptation combines Brechtian socio-political analysis with musical comedy. Steel Wasp is a young, vibrant physical theatre company. The challenge was to create an environment that located the play in terms of its literary origins and period, while offering dramatic space and mobile structures for the physicality of the company's storytelling. While always in the shadow of Newgate Gaol, poor old Moll spends a lifetime going up and down the social ladder. The show, by contrast, was a four-week run of one-night stands - so the set had to go up and down fairly easily too!'

Director: Simon Pirotte
Set Designer: Roger Maidment
Costume Designers: Roger Maidment,
Alex Morris and Sara Beadle
Lighting Designer: James Thurston
Choreographer: Julie Hobday
Assistant Designer: Beth Tearle
Photographer: James Thurston

Stefanos Lazaridis

The Greek Passion
Bohuslav Martinu
Text by Martinu after Nikos Kazantzakis

Bregenzer Festspielhaus, July 1999
Royal Opera House - London, May 2000

Stefanos Lazaridis: 'A village Passion
Play turns violent and the actor playing
Christ is stoned to death. The production
has a collage structure, linking together a
complex patchwork of small scenes,
encompassing village interiors and a bleak
mountainside. The design provides a
vertical series of small stages that might be
the rooms of village houses spread out on a
steep hillside. The separate platforms
suggest the stations of the cross.
Constructed around a vast, central tree
and linked by intertwining staircases, they
take the form of a double helix - the
arrangement of atoms at the heart of life
itself.

Director: David Pountney
Set Designer: Stefanos Lazaridis
Assistant Set Designer:
Matthew Deeley
Costume Designer:
Marie-Jeanne Lecca
Lighting Designer:
Davy Cunningham
Choreographer: Elaine Tyler-Hall
Conductors: Ulf Schirmer /
Charles Mackerras
Photographer (model):
Vassilis Skopelitis

Olivier Award for Best Opera
Production 2001

Madeleine Millar

Doctor Faustus
Edwin Morgan

TAG Theatre Company
Citizens' Theatre - Glasgow
Touring
September 1999

Madeleine Millar: 'The range of beautiful instruments used by the astrologers, astronomers, scientists and artists, such as Galileo, da Vinci, Holbein etc. - the types of object that would be at Doctor Faustus' disposal - became the inspiration for me to create a 3-D sculptural environment for the production. Some elements of the set transformed to provide us with projection screens: the telescope unrolls like a blind, the circular trap door opens, enabling us to juxtapose rare sensations of ancient and modern technologies.'

Director: James Brining
Set and Costume Designer: Madeleine Millar
Lighting Designer: Paul Sorley
Projections: Bevis Evans Teusa
Photographers:
Madeleine Millar and Kevin Low

Alison Chitty

Original Sin
Peter Gill

Crucible Theatre - Sheffield
May 2002

Alison Chitty: '*Original Sin* is a new version of the *Lulu* story, set in an all-male world, in the London and Paris of the 1890s. There are seven acts and six locations. We had to choose between how architecturally naturalistic to be and how expressive. We enjoyed creating what we call "poetic still lives". The design is a blank canvas which holds a series of poetic still lives that take us from location to location.'

Director: Peter Gill
Set and Costume Designer: Alison Chitty
Lighting Designer: Hartley T A Kemp
Photographer: Simon Annand

Michael Pavelka

Henry V
William Shakespeare

Royal Shakespeare Company
Royal Shakespeare Theatre
Stratford upon Avon
August 2000

Michael Pavelka: 'Our Henry - one of three conjoined productions dealing with patriotism, nationalism and violence. These images begin to say something about the energy that episodic plays of this sort need. We set out to keep the ensemble performers as mobile and accessible to the audience (and to themselves) as possible. A military company – in search of their lost saviour sovereign, national identity and mutual integrity - tells the story of "this star of England". Our platform stage, a prone memorial to the dead of Agincourt, offered up an assortment of memorabilia and paraphernalia, oddly constructed from an imaginary, army surplus glory hole.'

Director: Edward Hall
Set and Costume Designer: Michael Pavelka
Lighting Designer: Ben Ormerod

Christopher Richardson

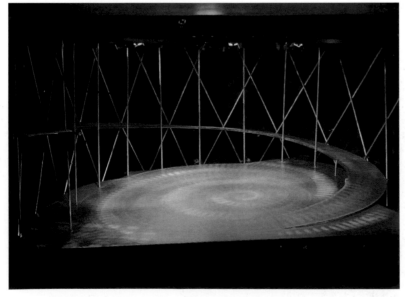

White Folks
Ray Shell, Dollie Henry and Paul Jenkins

WFC Ltd
The Pleasance Theatre - London
May 2002

Christopher Richardson: 'Words emerge from the text, conjuring up ideas and forms. The planet was a beautiful place before we came to it and will be beautiful when we have left it.'

Director: Ray Shell
Set Designer: Christopher Richardson
Set built by Will Jackson in the
Pleasance Theatre Workshops
Costume Designers: Tilly Colaco and
Carolyn Wilson
Lighting Designer: Matt Britten
Choreographer: Dollie Henry

Katy Tuxford

Macbeth
William Shakespeare

*The Marlowe Society
Cambridge Arts Theatre
February 2002*

Katy Tuxford: 'This production had an ageless setting, with influences from a barbaric and brutal age. The set remains modern while the costumes are reminiscent of Celtic, Anglo-Saxon times; their colours and textures complement the set. I used the cold, rigid feel of steel to help create a multi-layered construction that could be many things: interior, exterior, wasteland, castle and finally, hell. Ladders were built into the set so that actors could climb on to and into it in many different ways, then disappear into the darkness. I used the considerable depth of the stage and behind the cage-like frame, large, overlapping gauze screens worked as masking panels. In the final scenes, they were slowly illuminated from behind to reveal previously unseen skeletal trees.'

*Director: Ben Naylor
Set and Costume Designer: Katy Tuxford
Lighting Designer: Mark Willey
Choreographer: Anna Morrissey
Music: Jon Boden*

Sophia Lovell Smith

Mushroom Man
Hannah Beecham

*The Hungry Grass Theatre Company
Touring
June 2000*

Sophia Lovell Smith: 'How could I build a skeleton for this warped underworld? Raw surfaces, bruised flesh, peeling skin, erupting fungi, hidden gills. Mushrooms oozed through the floorboards and fibre optics wound through the bookcase, suggesting Mycelia.'

*Director: Rosamunde Hutt
Set and Costume Designer:
Sophia Lovell Smith
Lighting Designer: Ceri James
Composer and Music Director:
Hettie Malcolmson
Photographer: Philip Carr*

Robin Don

Blunt Speaking
Corin Redgrave

Minerva Theatre - Chichester
July 2002

Robin Don: 'In this one-man show, Anthony Blunt, Cambridge don, MI5 agent, KCVO, KGB spy, a dedicated Communist and art adviser to the Queen is played by the author. We see him becoming the focus in his own picture of events surrounding Mrs Thatcher's declaration of his treachery. We sense the betrayal that he feels by a country he loves, by the Queen and even by Stalin himself. The play explores the intimacy of Blunt as a prisoner in his own home as well as the breadth of him as a player on the world stage.'

Director: Mark Clements
Set and Costume Designer: Robin Don
Lighting Designer: Chris Ellis

Fiona Watt

The Trestle at Pope Lick Creek
Naomi Wallace

Traverse Theatre - Edinburgh
February 2001

Fiona Watt: 'A 1930s, small-town America in the grip of the Depression. As the nightly train hurtling across the trestle breaks through stagnation, so the arc breaks through the proscenium, hanging perilously over the audience.
Trestle turning into track, it symbolises an energy and a life force to the young people at the centre of the story that is now latent in the adults around them.'

Director: Philip Howard
Set and Costume Designer: Fiona Watt
Lighting Designer: Renny Robertson
Photographer: Kevin Low

Symbolic statements

Much of the work in this section is design for opera, where the audience is allowed more time to decode the elaborate, pictorial juxtapositions and sign systems presented by the designer.

British designers and creative teams using this vocabulary are in demand in opera houses across the world. The designs featured in this section make maximum use of symbol and metaphor. They use formalism, artificiality and surrealism to frame worlds-within-worlds, while seducing us with vivid colour and the scale of their ideas and realisation.

Many of these designs make the ordinary extraordinary through re-scaling;[1] through sheer force of numbers[2] and through surreal juxtaposition.[3] To be effective, the symbolic statement design or 'concept' production must be a complete piece of work, which is visually choreographed throughout and is therefore reliant upon close collaboration between directors, designers and lighting designers.[1,4,5]

Architectural styles are also a feature of the symbolic statement design. They create formal, almost alienating, environments for isolated objects and figures, that are examined and contemplated as though in a gallery environment.[6]

While still seen by a relatively small proportion of the theatre-going public, this work is hugely influential in the vocational theatre design courses.

1 Antony McDonald and Richard Jones, Bregenz Festivals p82-3
2 Ian MacNeil, Afore Night Comes p81
3 Richard Hudson, Tamerlano p74
4 Anthony Clark, Patrick Connellan, Tim Mitchell, Saint Joan p84
5 Graham Vick, Richard Hudson, Jennifer Tipton, Mozart/da Ponte operas p70
6 Ian MacNeil, Il ritorno d'Ullisse p80

Richard Hudson

Cosi fan tutte,
Le nozze di Figaro,
Don Giovanni
Wolfgang Amadeus Mozart.
Texts by Lorenzo da Ponte

Glyndebourne Festival Opera - Sussex
May 1998, May 2000, July 2000

Richard Hudson: 'Each of the three
Mozart/da Ponte operas was presented in
the same "room" - empty for *Cosi*, cut up
and partially obscured by gauze screens
for *Figaro*, invaded by an avalanche of
mud for *Don Giovanni*.'

Director: Graham Vick
Set and Costume Designer: Richard Hudson
Lighting Designer: Jennifer Tipton
Photographer: Mike Hoban

Paul Brown

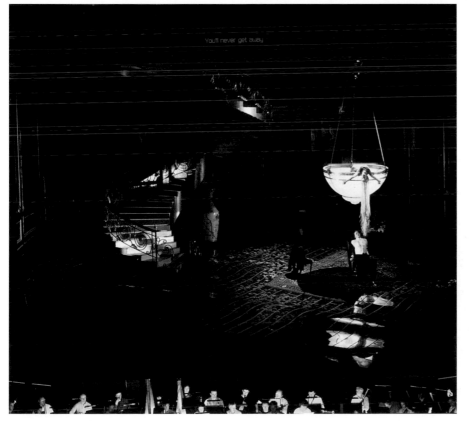

Pelléas et Mélisande
Claude Debussy
After Maeterlinck

Glyndebourne Festival Opera - Sussex
May 1999

Paul Brown: 'When my grandmother died, she was buried next to a grave on which had been placed a glass dome filled with wax flowers. As a child I was fascinated by those dead flowers, trapped under glass.'

Director: Graham Vick
Set and Costume Designer: Paul Brown
Lighting Designer: Matthew Richardson
Assistant Designer: Ros Coombes
Photographer: Mike Hoban

Will Bowen

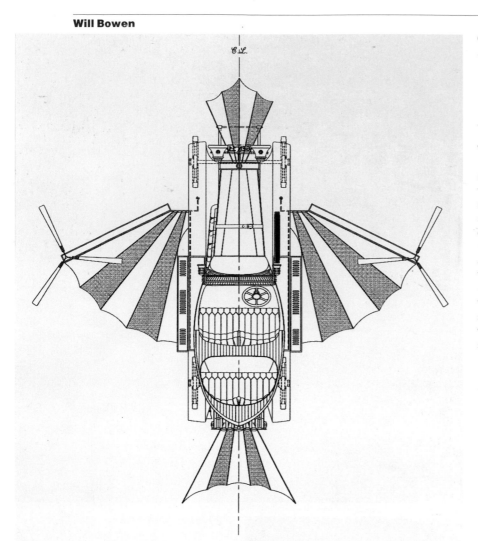

Chitty Chitty Bang Bang
Jeremy Sams, Richard M. Sherman,
Robert B. Sherman

Chitty (UK) Ltd.
London Palladium
April 2002

Will Bowen: 'The car - Chitty Chitty Bang Bang - is an iconic feature of the 1968 movie. For the 2002 production, the skin of the car had to be reproduced in lightweight materials. Working from photographs, old sketches and a Corgi toy, I drew the shape of the car's bodywork as traditional 2D plans and elevations for designer approval. From these I developed sections through the body shape, which were printed full size and pasted on to plywood, then cut out and slotted together to give a skeletal, 3D form. The gaps were in-filled with polystyrene and sculpted to give a solid maquette for the fibreglass mould.'

Director: Adrian Noble
Set and Costume Designer: Anthony Ward
Lighting Designer: Mark Henderson
Choreographer: Gillian Lynne
Technical Set Designer: Will Bowen
Engineering: Howard Eaton Lighting Ltd.
Sculpting and Fibreglass:
Stephen Pyle Workshop
Scenic Artist: Chris Clarke

Rob Batterbee

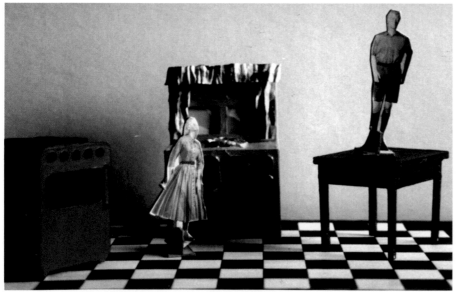

Big Boys Don't Cry
Peter Machen

Negativequity
Touring
July 2002

Rob Batterbee: 'This piece explores domestic violence towards men.
The design is based around a 1950s-style home, where everything is perfect.
The traditional view of the kitchen is used as a visual metaphor; exaggerating the size of the units. The woman is seen to dominate. The units move around the chess board floor making the characters disorientated, like pawns in a power struggle. The performance progresses to total meltdown.'

Directors: Peter Machen and Rebekah Fortune
Set and Costume Designer: Rob Batterbee
Lighting Designer: Bruno Edwards

Simon Holdsworth

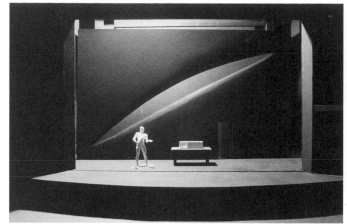 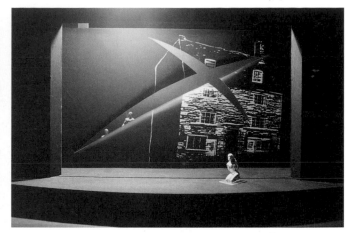

Ritual in Blood
Steven Berkoff

Nottingham Playhouse
June 2001

Simon Holdsworth: '*Ritual in Blood* is Steven Berkoff's first play and is different to the style of writing he is now famous for. It has 26 scenes and is based on historical events: the story is of the expulsion of Jews from 13th-century England. A family is falsely accused of cutting and bleeding a small boy at Passover and the house is ransacked. The design reflects this with gigantic knife wounds cut across large canvas flats. Although the canvas is two dimensional, the cuts turn inwards and characters are visible behind, making it a three-dimensional object on stage.'

Director: Timothy Walker
Set and Costume Designer: Simon Holdsworth
Lighting Designer: Zerlina Hughes

Robin Don

Turandot - the ballet
Giacomo Puccini
Additional music and orchestration by Huang Qiuyuan

Guangzhou Ballet
Friendship Theatre - Guangzhou, China
June 2002

Robin Don: 'Puccini's fantasy, set in a downtrodden China and re-orchestrated for dance. As the full moon displays its splendour, it revolves to reveal that it is, in fact, the rear of a huge skull, depicting Turandot's realm of death. The skull splits open to reveal a massive gong. The dazzlingly happy ending is enhanced when the skull revolves once more and transforms into a burnished golden orb of joy.'

Choreographer: Andrè Prokovsky
Set and Costume Designer: Robin Don
Lighting Designer: Liu Qing

Paul Edwards

Orfeo ed Euridice
Christoph Willibald Gluck
Text by Ranieri da Calzabigi

Opéra National du Rhin - Strasbourg
October 2002

Paul Edwards: 'The three locations of this opera are earth, hell and heaven. I wanted the earth location to be somewhere we could all recognise - the ubiquitous city - a Gotham City. The opera opens with Orfeo mourning Euridice's death. A New York taxi cab is slowly raised off the body of Euridice. Half the chorus are onlookers - bystanders in the city. The other half are set into niches in a three-storey wall watching like people from a high-rise building or as if they were the ashes of the dead in the niches of a crematorium wall.'

Director: Michael McCaffery
Set and Designer: Paul Edwards
Lighting Designer: Bruno Poet

Richard Hudson

Tamerlano
George Frederick Handel
Text by Agostino Piovene
after Jacques Pradon

Maggio Musicale Fiorentino
Teatro alla Pergola - Florence
May 2001

Richard Hudson: 'The set was a white semi circle punctuated by seven white doors. To symbolise the tyranny of Tamburlaine, a giant globe dominated by a naked foot was suspended in the centre, sometimes nearly touching the floor, almost crushing Bajazet, sometimes high up, almost out of sight.'

Director: Graham Vick
Set and Costume Designer: Richard Husdon
Lighting Designer: Matthew Richardson
Photographer: Robert Workman

Charles Cusick Smith

Il Trovatore
Giuseppe Verdi
Text by Salvatore Cammarano after Gutiérrez

Lo Productions and Hong Kong Culture and Leisure Services
Grand Theatre, Cultural Centre - Hong Kong
September 2001

Charles Cusick Smith: 'A divided circle represents the broken unity of the two brothers. The two half segments created different spaces to suggest internal and external scenes. A suspended moon traversed the full width of the back of the stage, indicating the passage of time.'

Director: Lo Kingman
Set and Costume Designer:
Charles Cusick Smith
Lighting Designer: Billy Chan
Choreographer: Susan Street

Joe Vaněk

Lady Macbeth of Mtsensk
Dmitri Shostakovich
Text by Preis and Shostakovich after Leskov

Opera Ireland
The Gaiety Theatre - Dublin
November 2000

Joe Vaněk: 'This Lady Macbeth kills for love. On the day of her husband's departure on business, Sergei, a new labourer, arrives. This scene shows the servants' farewell to the master.
The design's focus was drawn from Soviet film posters of the 1920s and 1930s - harsh angles, sharp colours and simplistic images.

Director: Dieter Kaegi
Set and Costume Designer: Joe Vaněk
Lighting Designer: Paul Keogan
Choreographer: Liz Roche

Stefanos Lazaridis

Lohengrin
Richard Wagner

Festspielhaus Bayreuth - Germany
July 1999

Stefanos Lazaridis: 'Wagner called *Lohengrin* his "blackest tragedy". Others have commented, "perhaps the only tragedy". This was the pervading mood for the production. We searched for an unsentimental realisation of Wagner's romantic universe; we produced a windswept, barren landscape awaiting redemption, visited by dreams and visions. In working on it we discovered it was a piece constructed around a labyrinthine series of dualities: How to reconcile this play of opposites? How to embody them into an acting style, discharge them into the lighting, sew them into the costumes, mould them into the props? An active battle of thesis and anti-thesis harmonised into a *gesamtkunstwerk* was our aim.'

Director: Keith Warner
Set Designer: Stefanos Lazaridis
Assistant Set Designer: Matthew Deeley
Costume Designer: Sue Blane
Lighting Designer: Manfred Voss
Conductor: Antonio Pappano
Photographer: Vassilis Skopelitis

Marie-Jeanne Lecca

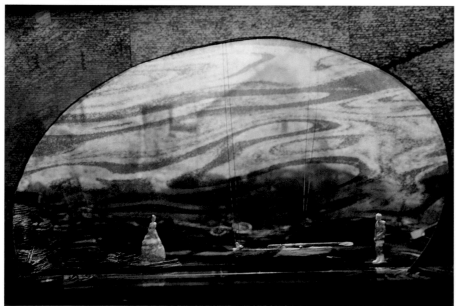

Director: Francesca Zambello
Set and Costume Designer:
Marie-Jeanne Lecca
Lighting Designer: Mark McCullogh
Conductor: Graeme Jenkins
Photo Credit: Dallas Opera

Thérèse Raquin
Tobias Picker
Text by Gene Scheer after Émile Zola

Dallas Opera
with l'Opéra de Montréal and San Diego Opera
Dallas Opera
December 2001

Marie-Jeanne Lecca: 'The opera is based on Émile Zola's powerful novel. Thérèse and her portrait painter lover, Laurent, murder her husband by drowning him. His ghost returns to haunt them to their graves. The production is set in the original period, but there is a continuous mixture of realistic detail and visual metaphor: on one hand, the domestic melodrama, on the other the aquatic element that washes away all contours and carries everything away with its flow. Its swirling moves are picked up by the set, the oval proscenium, surrounding flotsam and "water" curtain, while for the ghost scene real water flooding the bedroom wall washes out the colours of the husband's portrait - a putrid, rotting green versus the sepia tones of an old photograph.'

Peter Ruthven Hall

The Turn of the Screw
Benjamin Britten
Text by Myfanwy Piper after Henry James

Britten Pears School for Advanced
Musical Study
Snape Maltings Concert Hall - Aldeburgh
October 2000

Peter Ruthven Hall: 'Whereas Henry James suggests the ghosts are in the mind of the psychotic governess, Britten gives them a voice. But are they real or imaginary? By defining the areas around the main platform as the domain of the ghosts, their presence is always felt: sometimes glowing out of the dark, at other times casting ominous shadows across the back wall. The children reach out to them ... In the interludes, a mobile of Miles and Flora's toys and suspended underclothes revolves ominously overhead.

I work in 2D on the computer and 3D in the model box at the same time. After discussions with the director, I think very carefully about the piece and then work in a burst of energy, often leaving the project for a while to reflect subconsciously on my approach. I find it quick and flexible to sketch on the computer. I use Vectorworks, which allows me to think in shapes and volumes, much as I would on paper. Objects can be shifted and rescaled quickly and without the need to redraw each time. I only work in two dimensions on the computer. Equally important is my work on the model. I get an instant response to my design ideas in three dimensions and the proportions in space. And whilst I feed ideas back into the 2D computer files, I have no desire to model in three dimensions in the computer.'

Director: John Lloyd Davies
Set and Costume Designer:
Peter Ruthven Hall
Lighting Designer:
John Lloyd Davies

Andrew Wood

Cold
Peter Straughan

The Ashton Group Contemporary Theatre
Touring
April 2001

Andrew Wood: 'A sculptural iceberg houses four psychopathic young men and their doctor as they search for some kind of redemption. The images in performance weave together the isolation of the individuals, of their world lost in a black void and of an iceberg in an Antarctic landscape.'

Director: Rachel Ashton
Set and Costume Designer: Andrew Wood
Lighting Designer: David Hill
Composer: Olly Fox
Photographer: Joe Hutt

Juliet Shillingford

Night Swimming
Mark Castle

Nuffield Theatre - Southampton
February 2002

Juliet Shillingford: 'With the challenge of designing for 16 short scenes, I took photographs of textures, water, bark, and bricks. I made large laser prints and applied them to simple shapes: a cylinder, a rectangle, a curved floor. Avoiding the insistent naturalism of a play about petty drug dealing, we focused on the love story behind it, by making something more simple, sculptural and universal.

Director: Patrick Sandford
Set and Costume Designer: Juliet Shillingford
Lighting Designer: Jenny Cane
Photographer: Gemma Mount

Juliet Watkinson

Jago's Box
Maggie Willett

Sheffield Theatres Education Department
Touring primary schools
October 2002

Juliet Watkinson: '*Jago's Box* presents the issues of individuals caught up in the brutalities of civil war and sectarianism. Jago is a lone boy survivor, a collector of fragments, whose only refuge from pain and confusion is silence. Graf is a lone woman, wrenched out of normality, whose compassion and humanity have been locked into ice.'

Director: Karen Simpson
Set and Costume Designer: Juliet Watkinson
Lighting Designer: Gary Longfield
Musical Director: Matthew Wood

Tanya McCallin

Tanya McCallin

Macbeth
Giuseppe Verdi
Text by Francesco Maria Piave after
Shakespeare

Mariinsky (Kirov) Opera
Mariinsky Theatre - St Petersburg
April 2001

Tanya McCallin: 'The vast and crumbling architecture of the Mariinsky's stage space is laid bare and exposed. A slate and lead floor, punctured by uplit openings to and from the underbelly of the "world" provides a cold, dark and forbidding landscape. An angular, bloodied steel shard dissects the space brutally, abstractly altering the dynamics. The witches have marked a chalk circle on the ravaged land; two rotting corpses hang, abandoned. Sharply focused lighting and a diffusing haze sculpt and define the human figure in space and drive the psychological and physical narrative. Simplified Jacobean costumes place the characters in 17th-century Scotland.'

Director: David McVicar
Set and Costume Designer: Tanya McCallin
Lighting Designer: Davy Cunningham
Photographer: Natasha Razina

Ian MacNeil

Il ritorno d'Ulisse in Patria
Claudio Monteverdi
Text by G Badoaro

Bayerische Staatsoper
Prinzregententheater - Munich
July 2001

Ian MacNeil: 'The opera is about loss, recovery and growing old. We wanted epic and lonely spaces, each with a strong dynamic. We used elements of Third Reich architecture because the Trojan War also feels like another last gasp of menopausal machismo.'

Director: David Alden
Set Designer: Ian MacNeil
Costume Designer: Gideon Davey
Lighting Designer: Simon Mills
Photographer: Wilfried Hösl

Afore Night Comes
David Rudkin

Young Vic - London
September 2001

Ian MacNeil: 'The play is set in a pear
orchard that is both beautiful and
threatening. We represented nature with a
potting shed aesthetic: second hand ply
and 6,000 naked light bulbs. The play
builds to a horrific ritualistic murder.
We poured rain continuously down over the
lit bulbs until the moment of the killing when
the rain stopped and the light went out.'

Director: Rufus Norris
Set Designer: Ian MacNeil
Costume Designer: Joan Wadge
Lighting Designer: Rick Fisher
Sound Designer: Paul Arditti
Photographer: Keith Pattison

Antony McDonald, Richard Jones, Emma Ryott

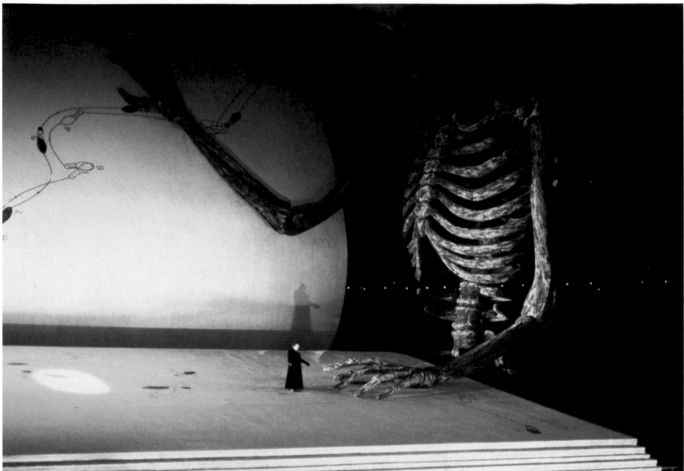

Ein Maskenball - A Masked Ball
Giuseppe Verdi
Text by Somma after Scribe and Auber

Bregenzer Festspiele (lake stage) - Austria
July 1999

Antony McDonald and Richard Jones
'Our design grew out of the obsession that
the character of King Gustavus has willed
the idea of his own death and his own
desire to choreograph it himself. Using his
best friend, the Prime Minister, and his best
friend's wife, the object of his erotic fixation,
he achieves his goal perfectly in a masked
ball where he presents himself as an
obvious target for the assassin's blade.
The simplicity of the open book serves as a
blank page against which characters are
easily seen and also as a teach-yourself
dance manual - read by a skeleton.'

Directors and Designers:
Richard Jones and Antony McDonald
Lighting Design: Wolfgang Göbbel
Co-Costume Designer: Emma Ryott
Choreographer: Philippe Giraudeau
Photographer: Karl Forster

La Bohème

Giacomo Puccini
Text by Giacosa and Illica after Henri Mürger

Bregenzer Festspiele (lake stage) - Austria
July 2001

Antony McDonald and Richard Jones:
'The set explored the myth of the lotus
eaters: an island inhabited by the young,
dedicated to pleasure. We wished to
create a city, a society, without using
conventional architecture that would dwarf
the performers; at the same time it had to
be Paris. We used the postcards on the
stand and the matches on the table to give
clues to location.'

Emma Ryott: 'We used a mixture of
modern fashion and retro 60s references.
The Bregenz stage is so large that we
needed to heighten the designs using an
almost graphic format of strong colour and
simple, readable silhouettes. We wanted
the principal characters to be down-beat
and realistic to emphasise their difference
from the guests and to identify them easily.'

Directors and Designers:
Richard Jones and Antony McDonald
Associate Costume Designer: Emma Ryott
Lighting Design: Wolfgang Göbbel
Choreographer: Philippe Giraudeau
Photographer: Karl Forster

Ruari Murchison

Nativity
Peter Whelan and Bill Alexander

Birmingham Repertory Theatre
December 1999

Ruari Murchison: '*Nativity* was a celebratory play for the end of the century. A fundamental, sculptural shape - the circle - was a visual symbol for the production. A steeply raked circular disc, surrounded by an outer raked rim, formed the performing area. These in turn were mounted on concentric floor revolves. Revolution of either disturbed an initial alignment, creating the many different locations required. The performers could work above, below and under the discs that were radially supported by ancient brick pillars. At the end of the piece, the revolves were aligned as at the beginning, forming a steeply raked circular stage - the world temporarily at peace.'

Director: Bill Alexander
Set and Costume Designer: Ruari Murchison
Lighting Designer: Tim Mitchell
Choreographer: Pat Garrett

Patrick Connellan

Saint Joan
George Bernard Shaw

Birmingham Repertory Theatre
May 2000

The trial of Saint Joan

Patrick Connellan: 'We tried to express the enormous power of the state and the established church against one audacious woman; the massed ranks of monks, cardinals and other clergy; the weight of an abused heaven propped up by the establishment teetering over the small shoulders of Joan.'

Director: Anthony Clark
Set and Costume Designer: Patrick Connellan
Lighting Designer: Tim Mitchell
Photographer: Tristram Kenton

'Come into my world'

All stage designs are created worlds, so what makes a 'world' as opposed to 'a performance environment'? Designs in this section set the performance in a particular time and place - historical, futuristic, a specific social or political environment, a mythical or fairytale world.[1]

The audience is invited to share the experience of a wrap-around world rather than being asked to observe. It is also invited to accept what is being presented, distanced neither by framing devices nor by performers stepping out of character. We are not asked mentally to fill in the gaps left by a minimal staging structure or token costumes.

Edges are important to complete worlds. Where does the performance space end and the audience begin? The auditorium may be included into the design concept; the floor of the set reaching under the front rows of the seating. Designs may be completed by ceilings and imagery offstage, which draw the audience into seemingly limitless constructions.

The lighting may also suggest a world outside, with strong shadows and patterns.

The world may be a bare but unified space,[2] or it may be composed from an assembly of furniture, props or objects.[3] Line structures are generally filled in, and surfaces and their treatments are important, with paint effects, texturing, textiles and colour, all used to unify the world. Costumes and props contribute vital information to the completeness of these designs, helping the audience to believe in the characters.

There are several designs for comedy in this section.[4,5] These perhaps best exemplify the 'complete world' design in which we, the audience, can recognise idiosyncrasies and foibles of our own worlds and join with the performers in commenting upon them.

1 Alistair Livingstone, I a Bayadère p86
2 Peter McKintosh, The Handmaid's Tale p94
3 David Burroughs, Mr Paul p98
4 Roger Glossop, House & Garden p99
5 Richard Foxton, The Importance of Being Earnest p103

Alistair Livingstone

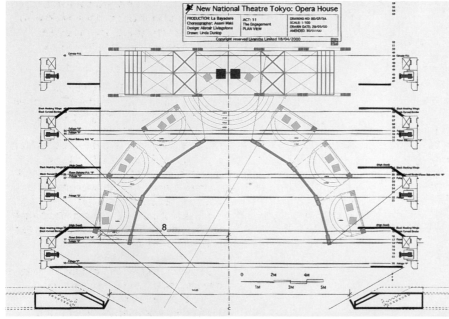

La Bayadère

Choreography by Marius Petipa
Revised by Asami Maki
Music by Leon Minkus, orchestrated by
John Lanchberry

New National Theatre Ballet Company
Opera Theatre, New National Theatre - Tokyo
November 2000

Alistair Livingstone: 'The computer
influenced the design process, helping to
create a new and interesting, interactive
dynamic between my work in the studio
and the production office at the theatre and
the manufacturers in Tokyo. The scenery
designs were created in 2D on the desktop
and then printed on to card as the basis for
a three-dimensional 1:50 scale model.
Although the computer assisted me to
discover a new design method, it is only a
tool. It was still not until the curtain rose and
the scenic space became alive with
dancers, music and light that the transition
from 2D to 3D is complete.'

Producer/Choreographer: Asami Maki
Production Designer: Alistair Livingstone
Scenery Supervisors:
Noboyuki Ito and Masato Sakamoto
Scenery Manufacture: Toho Workshop
Associate Lighting Designer: Mutsumi Isono
Photographer: Hidemi Seto

Emma Ryott, Robert Jones , Ian Sommerville

Manon Lescaut
Giacomo Puccini.
Text by Praga, Oliva and Illica after Prévost

Göteborgsoperan - Gothenburg
February 2002

Emma Ryott: 'Designing two productions of *Manon Lescaut* so close together (ENO, page 12, and then Gothenburg) I wanted to create a completely different world for Gothenburg. We opted for the turn of the 20th century. The metal and glass architecture of the setting was echoed in the colour palette: greys, blues, dusty pinks and purples. As the opera progressed, the colour gradually bleached out of the costumes to reach a dark and brooding monotone world which underlined the lovers' despair and the isolated desert setting, devoid of all colour.'

Robert Jones: 'As Manon leaves, deported on a prison ship for America, we see only a section of a huge steel hull. On to this bleak and grim vessel the prisoners slowly file as they set about their final journey. A torrential downpour leads us into Act IV (traditionally set in a desert) as the perfect world of Manon slowly destructs around her. The elegant symmetry of the world in which she began her journey (the railway station, Geronte's chateau) is reduced to ruins.'

Ian Sommerville: 'This production was never intended to make any pseudo-political statement or social comment. It was simply devised to stimulate the senses and give pleasure.'

Director: Vernon Mound
Set Designer: Robert Jones
Costume Designer: Emma Ryott
Lighting Designer: Ian Sommerville
Choreographer: Anthoula Papadakis
Photographer: Ingmar Jernberg

Jamie Vartan

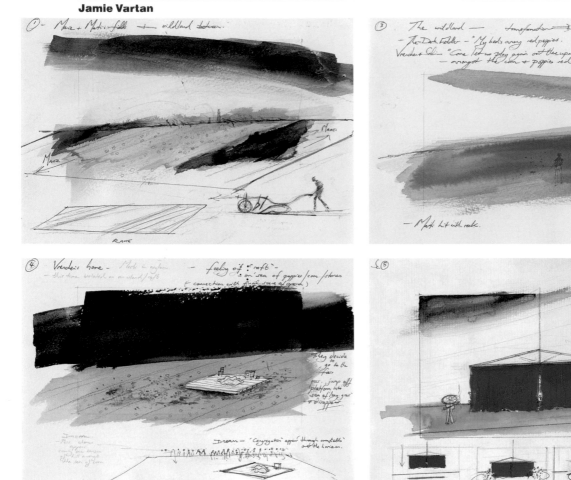

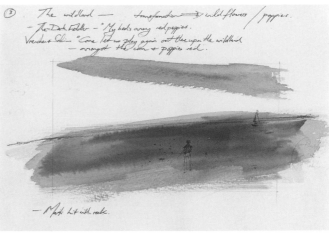

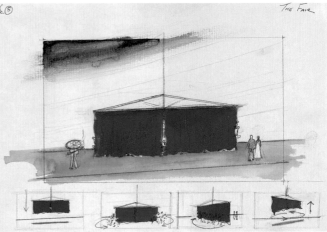

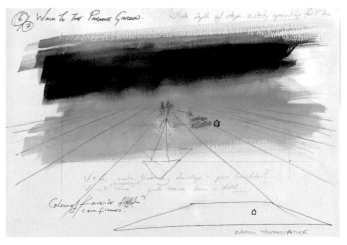

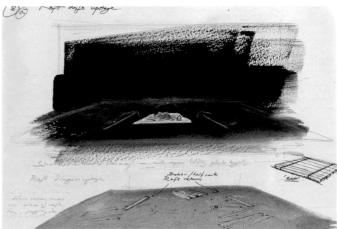

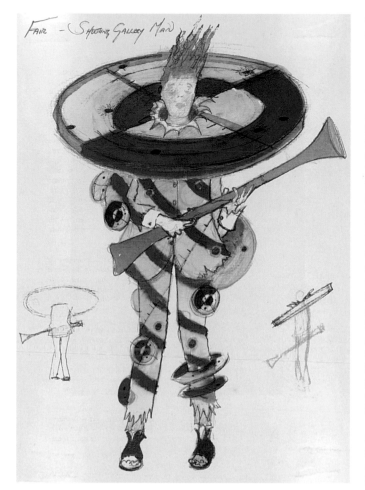

A Village Romeo and Juliet
Frederick Delius
Text by Delius after Gottfried Keller

Teatro Lirico di Cagliari - Sardinia
April 2002

Jamie Vartan: 'Two neighbouring farmers are slowly ploughing strips off either side of the wild land that separates them, but which their children use as a playground. The ensuing land dispute leads the two fathers to sever all ties, but the children secretly continue their friendship and their journey to find love alone. Delius' music is a line of continuous rich transformations - the home evokes a raft on a sea of corn from which they run away and laterthere is a real raft with a bed of corn, a square of land that they can finally call their own but that they know can never be permanent. Sali cuts the rope that binds it together, allowing them to die in each others' arms.
Along their journey, Vrenchen and Sali encounter a fair where characters appear from behind a revolving red curtain and parade to tempt them inside. The fair is one distinct and colourful memory of their travels, but even that flies away from them.'

Director: Stephen Medcalf
Set Designer: Jamie Vartan
Lighting Designer: Simon Corder
Choreographer: Maxine Braham

Ali Bell

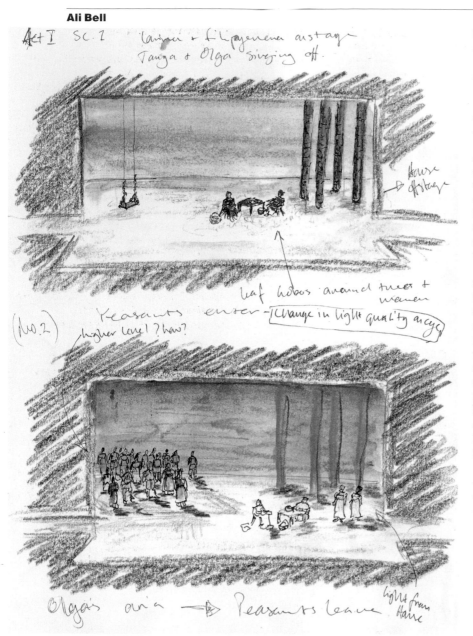

Eugene Onegin
Peter Ilitsch Tchaikovsky
Text by Tchaikovsky and Shilovsky, after Pushkin

Opera South East
Stag Theatre - Sevenoaks
April 2001

Ali Bell: 'This production was presented in a realistic and traditional way. The decision was the result of close discussion with the director and a thorough design process involving discussion of the piece, storyboarding, research into period, costume drawings, scale model and technical drawings. It is set in the early 19th century, in rural Russia and St Petersburg. The action frequently moves location, which required the design to suggest different environments. The basic elements were a permanent, triangular ramp upstage, three trees, a painted floorcloth, a front-lit cyclorama and for scenes placed inside, a gauze tracked across the centre stage. The lighting played an extremely important part, indicating time change, suggesting mood and locating the action. The cyc therefore became an indispensable part of the picture.'

Director: Orpha Phelan
Set and Costume Designer: Ali Bell
Lighting Designer: Kieron Doherty

Ian Sommerville

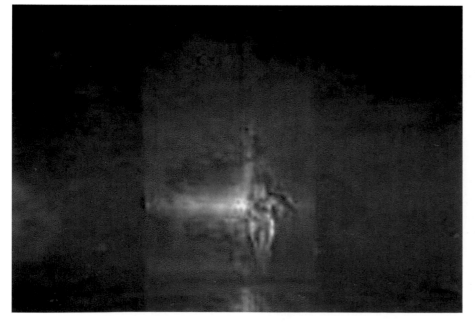

Greek
Mark-Anthony Turnage
Text by Jonathan Moore after Steven Berkoff

Royal Northern College of Music - Manchester
March 2000

Ian Sommerville: '*Greek* is based on the Steven Berkoff play of the same title which is, in turn, based on the Oedipus myth. It is a richly textured and visceral piece; ugliness and violence, beauty and tenderness in equal measures. The design reflects all these elements. The 2D to 3D connection comes from the real/unreal abstract and oh-so-very-hard-reality.'

Director: Jennifer Hamilton
Set Designer: Ian Sommerville
Costume Designers:
Jennifer Hamilton and Ian Sommerville
Lighting Designer: Ian Sommerville

David Cockayne

The Queen of Spades
Peter Ilitsch Tchaikovsky
Text by Modest Tchaikovsky after Pushkin

Royal Northern College of Music - Manchester
March 2002

David Cockayne: 'A storm-strewn, raked stage with the minimum of architectural elements for this fateful romantic story. The floor fissures for the entrance of the Countess' ghost, and remains broken. A chandelier falls to create a gaming table. The whole is watched over by a row of engraved female pilasters. The period moved from the late 18th century to the late 19th century.'

Director: Stefan Janski
Set and Costume Designer: David Cockayne
Lighting Designer: Acc McCarron
Choreographer: Bethan Rhys Wiliam

Isabella Bywater

I Puritani
Vincenzo Bellini,
text by Count Pepoli

Bayerische Staatsoper
Nationaltheater - Munich
May 2000

Isabella Bywater: '*I Puritani* takes place during the civil war in England (1640s). The opera is set in some kind of stronghold, used as a fortress by the Roundheads. I chose to create a building reminiscent of a church, as if it had been taken over and used as a military base. I wanted to create a sense of entrapment since those inside were comparatively secure but also unable to leave without great danger. By the time the opera begins, the war is nearly over and the people in the building have been there for several years. The community become quite intense and nervous.'

Director: Jonathan Miller
Set Designer: Isabella Bywater
Costume Designer: Clare Mitchell
Lighting Designer: Davy Cunningham
Photographer: Christopher Simon Sykes

Gemma Fripp

Il Re Pastore
Wolfgang Amadeus Mozart
Text by Metastasio

Classical Opera Company
Linbury Studio, Royal Opera House - London
March 2001

Gemma Fripp: '*Il Re Pastore* was originally intended as an oratorio. The design was a response both to the music and the ancient symbolism and magic within the piece. I wanted to capture the illusive quality of a desert landscape under a great expanse of sky and from this, to reveal magical elements to tell the story: a bubbling stream that turned to blood; beehives of honey representing greed and gluttony; an oasis of lush green grass that grew out of the sand. Creating theatrical moments in a context of heightened reality.'

Director: William Kerley
Designer: Gemma Fripp
Lighting Designer:
Jeanine Davies

Judith Croft

Falstaff
Giuseppe Verdi
Text by Arrigo Boito, after Shakespeare

Royal Northern College of Music - Manchester
March 2001

Judith Croft: 'Two of the opera's five scenes: the basic set of a stone floor and arched structures is revealed after the staircases, flags and fireplace which dressed the Garter Inn are stripped away. The garden of Ford's House is more Renaissance than Tudor with formal topiary and lead planters.

Maids beat mattresses from the windows and others hang out washing. Everyone is keen to know what is going on; groups gather to whisper and eavesdrop.
For the interior of Ford's House, the basic set has been softened and warmed by tapestries which fill the archways and cover the furniture. The river throws its reflection on the leaded lights of the Renaissance window and maids watch and whisper from the upper level.
The set retains its Italianate feel until the last act when the back wall flies out and Herne's Oak is revealed.'

Director: Stefan Janski
Set and Costume Designer:
Judith Croft
Lighting Designer: Nick Richings
Choreographer:
Bethan Rhys Wiliam
Conductor: Stephen Barlow

Peter McKintosh

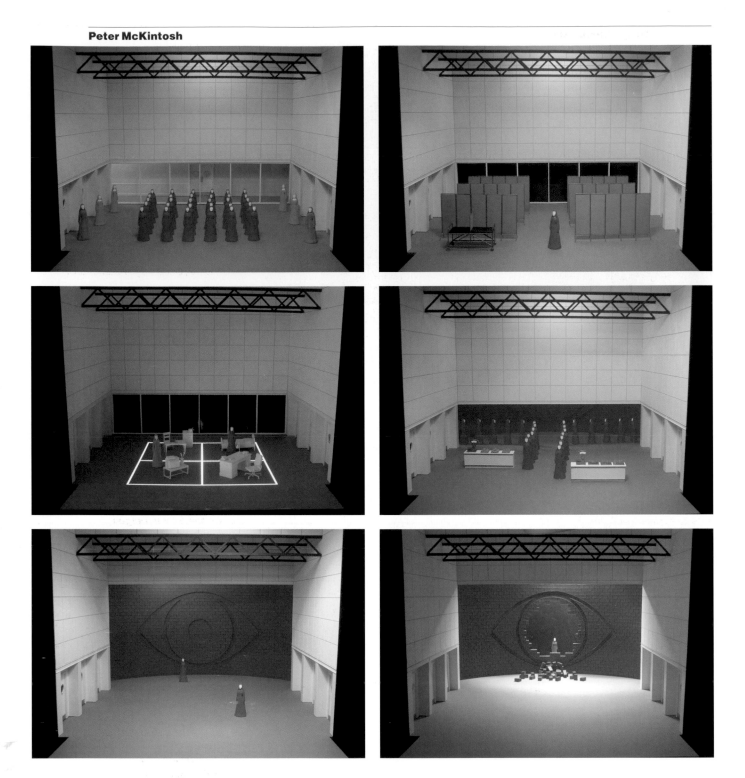

The Handmaid's Tale
Poul Ruders
Text by Paul Bentley,
based on Margaret Atwood's novel

Royal Danish Opera
Det Kongelige Teater - Copenhagen
March 2000

Peter McKintosh: 'Staging Poul Ruders' extraordinary opera, based on Margaret Atwood's vivid evocation of totalitarian blindness in 21st-century America, was a huge challenge. Atwood's images are very specific and often visual, but not necessarily theatrical. Therefore we had to try to find similar visual metaphors for this (literally) sterile world which would work on stage but still be true to the essence of the story. The relentless, filmic quality of the opera also dictated a visual shorthand to keep the piece flowing. For example, our "house" was a four-box neon floor panel with only essential furniture pieces, which revolved as if under a microscope.'

Director: Phyllida Lloyd
Set and Costume Designer:
Peter McKintosh
Lighting Designer: Simon Mills
Movement: Andrew George

Martyn Bainbridge

Under Milk Wood
Dylan Thomas

Theatr Clwyd – Mold
October 2001

Martyn Bainbridge: 'Dylan Thomas' wonderfully diverse characters evoke life in a Welsh village during the course of a single day. To emphasise the intimacy of the piece, we built the stage over part of the stalls of the theatre. The play has a sense of place and time so the set features a 3D, bird's eye view of the village and the sun shows the time of day throughout the action. The play is gently satirical, slightly sentimental, but always razor sharp.'

Director: Terry Hands
Designer: Martyn Bainbridge
Lighting Designer: Terry Hands

Simon Banham

**Nokon kjem til å komme
(Someone in going to come)**
Knut Vaage

Opera Vest
Den National Scene - Bergen
October 2000

Simon Banham: 'The opera centres on and revolves around an old house by the sea: the couple who buy the house, the old woman who died in the house and the son who sells the house. Much of the early drawing sought to reveal the presence of the house and how to animate it and the surrounding area through light, shadows and the objects that emanated from within. The house is the fourth character, a patient observer. The early drawings established a style that was pursued into the third dimension.'

Director: Michael McCarthy
Set and Costume Designer: Simon Banham
Lighting Designer: Ace McCarron

Matt Atwood

Eye Contact
Neil Monaghan

Theatre Machine
Riverside Studios - London
November 2000

Matt Atwood: 'Although the play explored both the on-stage and backstage world of table dancers, it focused on the latter to give insight into the dancers' real characters. The challenge was to heighten the "real" world, to give more depth and interest, without losing its real nature, while flattening the glamour of the club environment.'

Director and Choreographer: Izzy Many
Set and Costume Designer: Matt Atwood
Lighting Designers:
Matt Atwood and Nigel Catmur
Sound Designer and Composer:
Mike Woolmans
Photographer: Mark Douet, Celebrity Pictures

Keith Lodwick

The Little Prince
Matthew Peacock
Based on the story by
Antoine de Saint Exupéry

Streetwise Theatre Company
Linbury Studio, Royal Opera House - London
February 2000

Keith Lodwick: 'While travelling through space, the Little Prince encounters a number of characters all living in isolation on their own planets. The design evolved from Antoine de Saint Exupéry's original illustrations, appropriating their naive and pared down aesthetic. Locations and props were all created in miniature: the Sahara Desert, a field of corn, an aeroplane. When the Little Prince meets the King, the King's cloak covers the entire planet. The Little Prince emerges from its velvet folds.'

Director: Matthew Peacock
Set and Costume Designer:
Keith Lodwick
Choreographer: Darren Royston

Anthony Lamble

Sing Yer Heart Out for the Lads
Roy Williams

Transformations Season
Lyttelton Loft, National Theatre - London
May 2002

Anthony Lamble: 'The setting is the King George Public House, south west London, 7th October 2000 (the day of England's defeat by Germany in the World Cup qualifier). The flexible seating configuration enabled us partially to enclose the stage and extend the playing area diagonally across the theatre. This gave us sufficient width to separate areas of simultaneous action which occur between television screen, bar, football game, pool table and toilet. The different levels helped define the parameters of each locality and enabled us to maximise sightline potential: permitting a clear view of a scene performed upstage in the toilets, while characters downstage play pool. A naturalistic realisation of the pub environment reinforced the reality of the unfurling drama.'

Director: Simon Usher
Set and costume Designer: Anthony Lamble
Lighting Designer: Steve Barnett

Neil Irish

The Man Who Was Thursday
G K Chesterton

Red Shift Theatre Company
Bridewell Theatre - London
February 2001

Neil Irish: 'To bring Chesterton's fantastical story to the stage, many theatrical devices were used: puppets, disguises, changes of scale, models and masks. A crowd of 2D cut-out anarchists became the London skyline, their top hats piping smoke, small lights gently glowing, creating windows, doors and smokey alleyways.'

Director: Ben Harrison
Set and Costume Designer:
Neil Irish
Lighting Designer:
Jonathan Holloway
Composer: Philip Pinsky
Photographer: Gerald Murray

David Burrows

Mr Paul
Tankred Dorst

*Contemporary Stage Company
The Old Red Lion - London
October 2001*

David Burrows: 'Set in reunified Germany, the isolated and stubborn Herr Paul lives with his eccentric sister in the derelict soap factory they have made their home. Their existence is turned on its head with the arrival of Helm, who has inherited the factory and has major plans to renovate the site and move the ageing siblings. This was scavenging design: roadside skips, demolition timber - recycling to an extreme; little expenditure on materials but very labour intensive.'

*Director: David Graham-Young
Set Designer: David Burrows
Costume Designer: Chrystine Bennett
Lighting Designer: David Burrows*

Stephen Brimson Lewis

High Society
Cole Porter

*Crucible Theatre - Sheffield
December 2001*

Stephen Brimson Lewis: 'The musical High Society requires an adaptable, fluid space that links the cool, elegant interiors of the Lord's mansion to the sun-dappled terrace and pool with its breathtaking views of Oyster Bay beyond.'

*Director: Fiona Laird
Set and Costume Designer:
Stephen Brimson Lewis
Lighting Designer: Tim Mitchell
Choreographer: Alex Reynolds
Photographer: Ivan Kyncl*

Kim Beresford

Missing
Reza de Wet

*White Bear Theatre Club - London
April 2002*

Kim Beresford: 'I wanted to give the actors the maximum space available and give the audience the impression they were entering directly into the poverty-stricken kitchen where the drama unfolds. The corrugated iron interior, with a suspended wooden ceiling, needed a functional trap door through which things were lowered, using a system of pulleys.'

*Director: Derek Goldby
Set and Costume Designer: Kim Beresford
Lighting Designer: Richard Williamson
Choreographer: Terry John Bates
Photographer: Laurie Asprey*

Fred Meller

Life with an Idiot

Adapted by the company from a Russian short story by Viktor Erofeyev

The Gate - London
September 2001

Fred Meller: 'Masha and I live in a clean, all-white space in fear of mess and dirt. Their self protective, sanitary, packaged world is challenged by the visceral, guts and nasty inner workings of an "idiot". Madness is the liberation of the id, the dark side, of doing the forbidden with our bodies, our food, our excretions and our minds; a celebration of its anarchic energy, joy and appalling danger. Originating from an initial storyboard of the short story, the Gate was transformed into a complete environment with an extremely low ceiling.

This was invaded by colour and texture, shit, piss, blood and semen in the language of food, sexuality in the language of flowers and an audience uncomfortable and delighted by voyeurism and at defiling the space.'

Director: Ben Harrison
Set and Costume Designer: Fred Meller
Lighting Designer: Natasha Chivers
Composer: Charlie Winston

Roger Glossop

House & Garden

Alan Ayckbourn

Lyttelton Theatre (House),
Olivier Theatre (Garden),
Royal National Theatre - London
July 2000

Roger Glossop: 'One play, one cast, two theatres and two settings: House (a major stately home) and Garden (one of the garden areas of the house). The play was performed in both theatres concurrently over the timescale of a day and concerned events and relationships in action between House and Garden - the actors travelling (sometimes running) from one theatre to another. Out of the house and into the Garden. Out of the Garden and into the House.'

Director: Alan Ayckbourn
Set Designer: Roger Glossop
Costume Designer: Christine Wall
Lighting Designer: Mick Hughes
Choreographer: Sheila Carter
Design Assistant: Ana Snawdon

Bunny Christie

Baby Doll
Tennessee Williams

Birmingham Repertory Theatre
Lyttelton Theatre, National Theatre - London
March 2000

Bunny Christie: 'The show opened with a pin point of light high up in the darkness. This grew like a camera shutter opening to a "close-up" of Baby Doll in her crib. Gradually, the other rooms were revealed, inch by inch, making the audience feel it was spying on the characters. Later, Baby Doll and Vicarro hurtle through the empty rooms in a crazy game of hide and seek. In Act II, the exterior set filled the stage and felt like a panoramic long-shot after the claustrophobia of the house. It is a dry, dusty, junk-filed yard full of washed up aspirations and ghosts of an affluent past. The car goes nowhere. The water pump leaks and the cotton gin is bankrupt. In one corner is a heavenly cloud of cotton leading to the sky, where Baby Doll and Vicarro can hide from her husband. Chris Davey's lighting changed the space from steamy, cotton-filled haze to expressionistic shadows and piercing shafts of light.'

Director: Lucy Bailey
Set and Costume Designer: Bunny Christie
Lighting Designer: Chris Davey
Music: Django Bates
Photographer: Ivan Kyncl

Alex Marker

Helen of Troy

Euripides, translated by Adonis Galleos,
Catherine Stevens and Toni Brown

Questors' Youth Theatre
The Questors' Theatre Studio - London
February 2001

Menelaus contemplates how to break into King
Theoklymenus' Palace

Alex Marker: 'The underlying theme of conflict between the Greek and Egyptian characters inspired me to create two distinct structures opposing each other across a traverse stage. At one end stood the Egyptian palace, solid and powerful; at the other, a scaffold structure shrouded in muslin - through which the audience enters - to reflect the more nomadic Greeks. This doubled as the tomb where Helen seeks sanctuary and as the sails from Menelaus' wrecked ship. For the finale, the higher level drapes flew upwards to reveal the Gods waiting to cast judgement.'

Director: Catherine Stevens
Set and Costume Designer: Alex Marker
Lighting Designer: Damien Lazell

Charlie Cridlan

The Front Page

Ben Hecht and Charles MacArthur

Bristol Old Vic Theatre School, New Vic Studio
July 1999

Charlie Cridlan: 'A criminal court press room in 1920s, in downtown Chicago. Assorted hacks hang around playing cards, waiting for the scoop on a public execution. It was important to create a highly naturalistic environment with a real sense of the outside: corridors leading off, the prison yard, the sense of a seventh floor room in a tall building.'

Director: Chris Denys
Set Designer: Charlie Cridlan
Costume Designer: George Naylor
Lighting Designer: Brian Smith

Patrick Connellan

A Midsummer Night's Dream

William Shakespeare

Shysters Theatre Company
Belgrade Theatre - Coventry
September 2001

Patrick Connellan: 'Away from authority and the oppressiveness of CCTV is the end of the motorway that leads into Athens. The Fairies live off the rubbish thrown from the city by the Mechanicals; discarded TVs broadcast the passion of Oberon and Titania's quarrel.'

Directors:
Richard Hayhow and Patrick Connellan
Set and Costume Designer: Patrick Connellan
Lighting Designer: Michael E Hall
Assistant Director: Lindi Ritter-Smith
Photographer: Ian Tilton

Lis Evans

Moll Flanders

Music by George Stiles
Lyrics by Paul Leigh. Original lyrics
by Claire Luckham and Chris Bond
based on a novel by Daniel Defoe

New Vic Theatre - Newcastle under Lyme
February 2000

Lis Evans: 'The cast of nine, playing more than 40 characters, wore basic white costume over which garments such as fichu, stock, sleeves or a bonnet were worn to depict different characters. The setting, costumes and props were entirely black, white and grey, with elements of galvanised steel and gold coins. There were subtle mixes of thin white voiles, paper, calico, ticking and textured upholstery fabrics.'

Director: Gwenda Hughes
Set and Costume Designer:
Lis Evans
Lighting Designer: Jo Dawson
Choreographer:
Beverly Edmunds
Musical Director:
Richard Atkinson
Sound Designer:
James Earls Davis
Photographer: Robert Day

Simon Holdsworth

The Secret Love-Life of Ophelia
Steven Berkoff

Green & Lenagan Limited
Assembly Rooms - Edinburgh
August 2001

Simon Holdsworth: '*The Secret Love-Life of Ophelia* is an exchange of love letters between Hamlet and Ophelia, the two characters from Shakespeare's play. Although the lovers never meet, they do in their imaginations. Writer and director Steven Berkoff was keen to have a simple set comprising only a floor and back wall. The "letter" setting keeps the audience's attention on the activity of writing, as Hamlet and Ophelia's movements become more animated. The 3D shape is deceptively 2D as it surrounds the characters on three sides.'

Director: Steven Berkoff
Set and Costume Designer: Simon Holdsworth
Lighting Designer: David Edwards

Richard Foxton

The Importance of Being Earnest
Oscar Wilde

*Lipservice Theatre Company
Co-produced with Library Theatre,
Manchester and Palace Theatre - Watford
Touring
June 2001*

Richard Foxton: 'The premise of this
production was that most of the company
had been detained by the local
constabulary. But they were expected to
arrive shortly. The remaining cast members
- Lady Bracknell and Gwendolen - would
therefore start the show off, playing Jack
and Algy, until the rest of the company
materialised. As each member arrived,
they took the parts of the next character on,
thus Jack played Lady Bracknell, and Algy,
Gwendolen. The whole thing was played
out against an enormous handbag. It was
closed for the first act and opened at the
beginning of the second to reveal the
country landscape. In the final act it was
climbed by the cast, fronted by furniture
made of books and then demolished in
the frenzied search for the "army lists".
The whole thing has a 1950s feel but
strayed backwards and forwards as
required.'

*Director: Lawrence Till
Set and Costume Designer: Richard Foxton
Lighting Designer: Ian Saunders
Composer: Mark Vibrans*

Nettie Scriven

Aesop's Fables
Adapted by Mike Kenny

*Sherman Theatre - Cardiff
May 2002*

Nettie Scriven:
'We three (writer, director, designer)
wanted the child to be at the centre of the
world, wanted to re-frame the view.
We created a canopy - a storytelling world -
placing the audience on the proscenium
stage, encircling them with two golden
domes. We played with viewpoints,
(looking up at the stars within the lace sky,
looking down at jewels sewn into shoes).
We played with scale,(sitting on the tiny
chair, standing on the tall chair, moving
from large to small dome). We changed the
eye level to that of a young child.'

*Director: Phil Clark
Set and Costume Designer:
Nettie Scriven
Lighting Designer: Chris Davies
Composer: Paula Gardiner
Photographer: Andrew Jeffery*

Dana Pinto

This Happy Breed
Noel Coward

BBC3 Ltd and Man in the Moon - London
June 2000

Dana Pinto: 'The story of the Gibbon family between the world wars brings to life the scenes depicted in an old family album. I created the effect of a living photograph by using a sepia colour scheme and ripping away the edges of the walls. The play is set in the same room from beginning to end, but between scenes the furniture is moved and utilised in new ways.'

Director: Helen Alexander
Set Designer: Dana Pinto
Costume Designer: Vanessa Crane
Lighting Designer: Steve Millar

Jessica Stack

The Blue Room
David Hare

Hull Truck Theatre Company
Touring
September 2001

Jessica Stack: 'Ten scenes with ten characters who meet and leave each other again. I wanted the set to reflect the play's circular, revelatory structure within the confines of a thrust stage. The multi-faceted set opened from within boxes and levels, allowing the many scenes to take place on one modular set, and retaining an element of surprise for the audience.'

Director: Kate Bramley
Set and Costume Designer: Jessica Stack
Lighting Designer: Graham Kirk

Naomi Wilkinson

Happy Birthday Mr Deka D
Biyi Bandele

Told by an Idiot
Traverse Theatre - Edinburgh
August 1999

Naomi Wilkinson: 'Three characters are sitting in a pub with time apparently suspended. Their disjointed, melancholic communications condemn them to endless repetition. By raking the floor from both sides into a central crack, I hoped to create a sense of imminent collapse - a catastrophe - while subsuming and entrapping the furniture and characters in a swamp of perpetual moment.'

Director: John Wright
Set and Costume Designer: Naomi Wilkinson
Lighting Designer: John McKenzie

David I Taylor

Wine in the Wilderness / Water
Alice Childress and Winsome Pinnock

The Tricycle Theatre - London
October 2000

David I Taylor: 'The cleverly matched double bill at the Tricycle moved a discussion about African-American identity from rhetoric to reality through the medium of art. Painters dealing with their heritage and the relevance of their history to modern times (the modern times of 1960s America in "Wine" and the Brit Art scene in "Water") brought the image from the canvas out on to the streets.
The lighting for the double bill placed the artists' studios into a limbo, touched by the realism of the streets outside, but elevated to a more dimensional and creative environment through colour, texture and contrast.'

Director: Nicolas Kent
Set and Costume Designer: Poppy Mitchell
Lighting Designer: David I Taylor

Haibo Yu

Dracula
Mac Wellman after Bram Stoker

UT Theatre, California State University
Sacramento
May 2001

Haibo Yu: 'Everybody's conception of Dracula is different. In this production, the panoramic landscape of Transylvania, Whitby and Castle Dracula have been transformed into an oil refinery. Pipes and hoses tangling above the acting space symbolise the blood vessels of a modern society. The universe is created by projecting images on to the floor instead of a conventional cyclorama.'

Director: Robin Henson
Set and Lighting Designer: Haibo Yu
Costume Designer: Bonnie Busick

Janet Vaughan

Black Box
Talking Birds

Talking Birds
Touring
September 1999

Janet Vaughan: 'A Gilliam-esque future where plane crashes supposedly don't happen: three forgotten, filed-away investigators file away the crash victims captured on numerous archived black box flight recorders. This neat existence is turned upside down by the arrival of a survivor, a real, 3D statistical anomaly bringing colour and chaos into their monochromatic world. Suddenly the filed away won't stay forgotten.
The possessions of hundreds of victims are escaping out of the drawers, encroaching on the space, turning the stage into a crash site, strewn with the wreckage of the investigators' lives as well as the forgotten victims.'

Director: Nick Walker
Set, Costume and Lighting Designer:
Janet Vaughan
Composer: Derek Nisbet

Animation : illumination

The interrelation of lighting and structure has its roots in the experimental work of Adolphe Appia and Edward Gordon Craig, shifting a 250-year preoccupation with lighting 2D painted scenery in favour of sculpting the figure and its environment.

Lighting and projection design are hugely influential aspects of contemporary performance. They embody the fourth dimension of Peter Brook's 'stage moving picture', transforming 3D space and structures, over time, using a wealth of devices that are impossible to represent in the illustration of a single moment.

While some lighting designers may design sets, others create the performance environment through light alone. [1] Elsewhere, set designers and visual artists working in performance choose to design their own lighting and introduce projection and digital media as elements of the set. [2,3,4]

Design for performance draws increasingly on the lighting techniques and treated image projection of live music performance, videos and DVDs. More affordable, sophisticated and easily controllable technology has greatly extended the possibilities for theatre designers who work across the boundaries of theatre, film and music.

Lighting designs visualised in a virtual world, on a laptop, can be translated into the full-scale beams of fixed or moving lights. Images made, or manipulated, on computer can also be transferred straight to performance in the form of large-scale projections. [5]

1 Neil Austin, A Prayer for Owen Meany p108
2 Janet Bird, Attempts on her Life p113
3 Lucinda Meredith, A Little Sexy Something in Between p113
4 Vivienne Schadinsky, London / My Lover p114
5 Arnim Friess, Life on Mars p115

Neil Austin

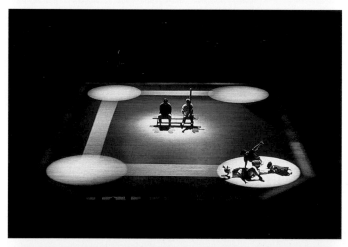

A Prayer for Owen Meany
Adapted by Simon Bent
from the novel by John Irving

Lyttelton Theatre, National Theatre - London,
June 2002

Neil Austin: 'The production's conceit of a
light, wooden floor, surrounded by black
masking, provided an empty space to be
transformed by acting and lighting alone.
The piece was a memory play condensed
from a 600-page novel into 78 scenes,
many of which overlapped. Lighting was
key to clarifying location and time as well
as mood and atmosphere.
The transformed auditorium allowed the
entire audience to look down on the stage
floor and so shapes of light projected on to
it were used to represent the different
locations. The time frame of narration
versus memory had to be clearly
distinguished. Discharge sources, hard-
focused into drop-spots were used to light
the narrator in the present, while the stage
was edged with a thin border of tungsten
light to represent the memory of the past.'

Director: Mick Gordon
Set and Costume Designer: Dick Bird
Lighting Designer: Neil Austin

Mark Jonathan

Powder
Clarinet Concerto by
Wolfgang Amadeus Mozart

Birmingham Royal Ballet,
Birmingham Hippodrome and
touring

Mark Jonathan: 'The spirits of the music come to life each time the music is performed. The lighting starts at dawn. In the second movement it moves to a sultry sunset and on to night. The ballet ends as morning returns.'

Choreographer: Stanton Welch
Set and Costume Designer: Kandis Cook
Lighting Designer: Mark Jonathan
Photographer: Bill Cooper

Ken Coker

Othello
William Shakespeare

Theatre Unlimited on tour
April 2002

Ken Coker: 'The Moor is almost invisible; the full moon and the candle burn at the same colour temperature; what waxes, what wanes? For the first time in five acts there is direct motivational light; previously there have been shifts of angle and slight movements of colour, with all the lighting instruments hidden from view by the picture postcard masking. The light thickens and pulls Othello and Desdemona to their fate as the moon pulls the tide.'

Director: Chris Geelan
Set and Costume Designer: Bridget Kimak
Lighting Designer: Ken Coker
Photographer: Bridget Kimak

Rick Fisher

Wozzeck
Alban Berg, after Büchner

Santa Fe Opera, USA
July 2001

Rick Fisher: 'The Santa Fe Opera Theatre is partially outdoors. The darkening sky and the open, upstage perspective of distant mountains creates a compelling backdrop for all opera performed there. Wozzeck traces the final deterioration of a soldier who is used as a medical guinea pig. As his mental state deteriorates, the world around him becomes more disjointed and sections of the set begin to tilt. The scene becomes increasingly surreal and the light uses gaps in the scenery to distress the picture. In the final scenes, colour becomes more intense as Wozzeck sees a blood red moon reflecting his inner turmoil at the murder of his mistress.'

Director: Daniel Slater
Set and Costume Designer:
Robert Innes Hopkins
Lighting Designer: Rick Fisher
Photographer: Robin Payne

Hansjorg Schmidt

Henry VIII
William Shakespeare, adapted by Phil Willmott

The Steam Industry
The Bridewell Theatre - London
June 2002

Act 1, scene 1: Cardinal Wolsey

Hansjorg Schmidt: 'Shakespeare's plays are a like a blank canvas. Written to be performed under daylight in a time not our own, they ask for a new world to be created. We wanted to set this in a modern world, recognisable through a strong visual style. The play tells the story of a young Henry's relationship with two strong women - Queen Katherine and Anne Boleyn - in a world unsure of itself. These themes drew us to *film noir* as a key reference point. The set was simple: two revolving doors that blended into the fabric of this striking venue (a Victorian swimming pool). Lighting was used both to create the world of the play and to cut through and define the three-dimensionality of the space, generating a multitude of locations and giving the word space to breathe.'

Director: Phil Willmott
Set and Costume Designer: Rosemary Flegg
Lighting Designer: Hansjorg Schmidt
Photographer: Sheila Burnett

David W Kidd

King Oedipus
Sophocles, translated by Kenneth McLeish

Nuffield Theatre - Southampton
September 2001

David W Kidd: 'Ti Green's setting for this *King Oedipus* incorporated both organic and geometric forms: strewn rocks, dark reflective walls, snow-peaked mountain tops and a moon peeping at us from upstage centre. A back projection screen upon which the sky, moon and mountain were printed, gave wonderful opportunities in the lighting to articulate the narrative and mood. The changing colour and intensity of the sky and moon engendered a powerful back light at climactic moments. Some scenes, mostly lit by a single source, created dramatic shadows, all helping build the tension for the crushing finale of Oedipus' fate.'

Director: Patrick Sandford
Set and Costume Designer: Ti Green
Lighting Designer: David W Kidd
Photographer: Gemma Mount

Michael E Hall

Macbeth
William Shakespeare

Everyman Theatre - Cheltenham
March 2001

Michael E Hall: 'Performed by a small
ensemble company working in a black box
setting, the production drew on the
animalistic imagery of the text.
Bold strokes of colour and unseen beams
of light captured the performer in space
and created the inner and outer worlds of
the Macbeths within the black box.
The lighting emphasised the physical
qualities of the actors' performances.
The lighting positions and techniques used
came from the world of dance lighting with
only slight modifications (low levels of
diagonal front lighting) for use in a text-
based production.'

Director: Sue Colverd
Set and Costume Designer: Sue Condie
Costume Designer: Ruth Sabin
Lighting Design: Michael E Hall

Fallen Angels
Devised by the company, text by Alex Jones
Music by Mike Longmoor

Shysters Theatre Company
Arts Alive Studio, Belgrade Theatre - Coventry
Touring
June 2000

Michael E Hall: 'The world is one of
angels, misfits and outcasts, false gods
and a young man's mum. The set, a flexible
space, monochromatic, geometrical with
alchemical allusions; the lighting, a poetic
response to the deep emotions and
psychological issues the piece explored.
Throughout the life of this devised
production, the lighting continually evolved
using a key series of elements - gobos,
colours, lighting positions and effects -
utilising the skills of a designer/operator
who toured with the production and
enabled the lighting to become another
member of the cast. As part of a devising
team I was given free rein to contribute
artistically to the production, adding a
dimension to the lighting that is not often
possible.'

Director: Richard Hayhow
Set and Costume Designer: Nettie Edwards
Lighting Designer: Michael E Hall
Movement: Rachel Karafistan

Lucinda Meredith

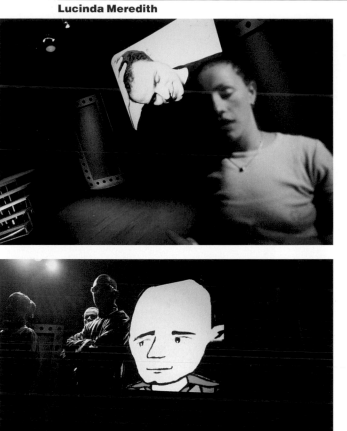

A Little Sexy Something in Between

Economical Truth
The Oval House - London
January 2000

Lucinda Meredith: 'This production mixed 3D action with 2D pre-recorded cartoon sequences. The result was a lively mix of cartoon alter egos and real life characters. The images were projected on a large back projection screen that could be masked using moving screens.'

Director: David Jubb
Set and Costume Designer: Lucinda Meredith
Lighting Designer: Sarah Ferguson
Film Animator: Timothy Nunn
Photographer: Timothy Nunn

Janet Bird

Attempts on her Life
Martin Crimp

George Bernard Shaw Theatre, RADA
London
June 2001

Janet Bird: 'The process of examination and re-examination took place in an austere environment of steel, concrete and brick. Visual information was reported and re-reported using close-circuit TV, reflection and projection.'

Director: John Adams
Set and Costume Designer: Janet Bird
Lighting Designer: David Bishop
Choreographer: Beverley Edmunds

Vivienne Schadinsky

London / My Lover
Devised by the company

Lightwork
ICA - London
January 2002

Vivienne Schadinsky: 'The show follows the daily routine of a man and a woman in London, using live and pre-recorded video projection. Six months earlier, members of the company captured images of London on a digital video camera. We then devised the show. I wanted a controlled 2D outdoor space that looks narrow, cool and grey. The performers are on two raised pedestals in front of a large, silk screen, providing four points of focus: two bodies, two images. The city is shown as a labyrinth, as something that can be experienced in its parts but not in its entirety. When the man and woman meet and become lovers, the screen drops and the stage fully opens up. It looks strange and seductive. With a large, flesh-coloured projection screen upstage, the space becomes 3D, undefined, warm and emotional.'

Director: Andy Lavender
Set and Costume Designer:
Vivienne Schadinsky
Lighting Designer: Sarah Brown
Video Design:
Detsky Forsyth Graffam
and David Barlia
Sound Design: Gregg Fisher

Arnim Friess

Life on Mars
Richard Williams

Legoland Denmark, California and Windsor
Lego Family Attractions International
March - June 2001

Arnim Friess: 'As 2D meets a 3D artform,
interesting friction happens. Sometimes
projection is just extended lighting with
more meaning attached. Or it can add
cinematic quality, become a virtual
character, switch visual style or the
perception of space in a second, shaped
along the forms of a set. *Life on Mars* - a
bricks-in-space spectacle at Legoland -
synchronised lighting with slide-projection
on a 17m x 3m Milky Way with dropped-in
video sequences. Tilting above the stage
into the auditorium, it enveloped set and
viewer with Martian landscapes, space
flights and vision screens to translate
Martian language to the multilingual
audience and to link in with special effects
like a red (confetti) dust-storm.'

Director: Richard Williams
Set and Costume Designer: Janey Gardiner
Lighting Designer: Arnim Friess
Choreographer: Sam Spencer-Lane
Montage: Arnim Friess from production
photography by Janey Gardiner

Nerissa Cargill Thompson

Mad Forest
Caryl Churchill

The Arden School of Theatre - Manchester
March 2002

Nerissa Cargill Thompson: 'Set in
Roumania during the 1989 revoution, this is
a piece of brief cinematic scenes. I used
grey 3D structures to create an austere and
abstract world. Lighting and gauze panels
allowed us to flick quickly between scenes,
catching moments of reality and emotion in
a world where everyone is hiding.'

Director: Paul Jaynes
Set and Costume Designer:
Nerissa Cargill Thompson
Lighting Designer: Richard G Jones

John Risebero

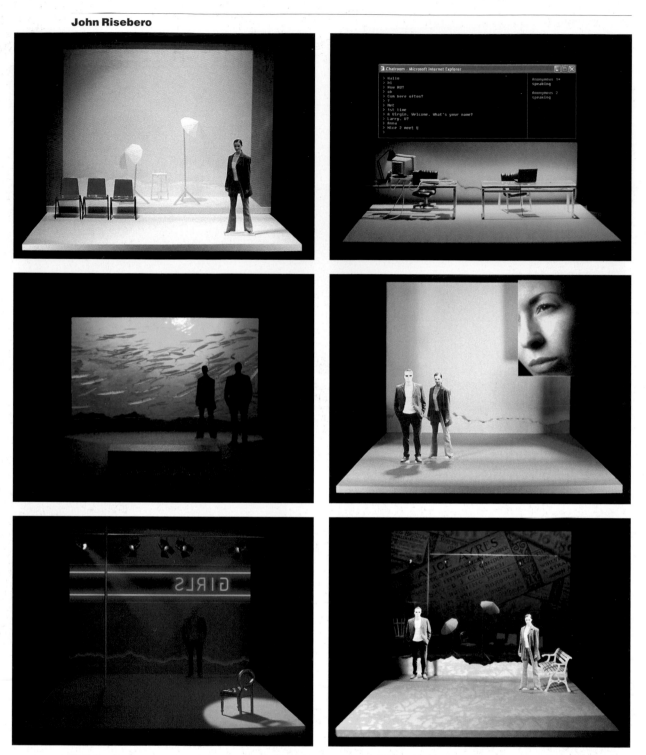

Closer
Patrick Marber

Epilogue Productions
ADC Theatre - Cambridge
July 2002

John Risebero: 'Closer explores themes
of sexual jealousy, desire and isolation. It is
slick, witty, modern and obscene, but also
painful, resonant and sad. The entire world
of the play is a small, clean, white box.
Video projection, slick scene changes, and
minimal use of furniture take us to 12
locations over four years. But this is a world
devoid of warmth. It is stark, clinical and
restricting. The final scene of the play sees
one of the characters, Alice, break free of
the box. The stage doubles in depth,
revealing memories of past events, as the
remaining three characters meet to share
the news of Alice's death - and liberation.'

Director: Patrick Nielsen
Set Designer John Risebero
Costume Designer: Robyn Wilson
Lighting Designer: Linda Ekholm

2D|3D

Biographies

Index of productions

Index of designers

Index of companies

Biographies

Liz Ascroft
After graduating from Wimbledon School of Art, Liz Ascroft won an Arts Council bursary to work at the Belgrade Theatre, Coventry. Her freelance work includes: *The Grapes of Wrath* (RADA, London); *Death and the Maiden, Alice's Adventures In Wonderland,* and *A Midsummer Night's Dream* (The Duke's, Lancaster); *'Tis Pity She's A Whore* and *Man in the Moon* (Liverpool Playhouse). Recent designs include: William Nicholson's *Katherine Howard* (Chichester Festival Theatre); Brian Friel's *Give Me Your Answer Do*, Philip Ridley's *Apocalyptica* (Hampstead Theatre, London); Kevin Hood's *So Special* and Abi Morgan's *Fast Food* (Royal Exchange, Manchester). At the Prague Quadrennial (1999), UNESCO awarded her a prize for promotion of the visual arts. Since then, she has designed Alan Plater's *Peggy For You* (Hampstead Theatre and Comedy Theatre, London and tour); Fiona Padfield's *Snapshots*, Simon Robson's *The Ghost Train Tattoo, As You Like It* and *Hedda Gabler* (Royal Exchange); Philip Ridley's *Vincent River*, and Steve Waters' *After The Gods* (Hampstead Theatre); Billy Roche's *Cavalcaders* (The Tricycle Theatre, London); Conor McPherson's *Dublin Carol* and Ronald Harwood's adaptation of *See You Next Tuesday* (The Gate, Dublin); Brian Friel's *The Bear* and *Afterplay* (The Gate, and Spoleto Festival, Charleston, South Carolina); and Harold Pinter's *One For The Road* and *A Kind of Alaska* (The Gate, and The Lincoln Centre, New York).

Elroy Ashmore
Elroy Ashmore studied design with Motley on the ENO Design Course and went on to assist various eminent designers in opera, ballet and drama. He became an assistant designer at the Young Vic, London and the Thorndyke Theatre, Leatherhead before heading design teams at the Belgrade Theatre, Coventry and the Haymarket Theatre, Basingstoke. He now works freelance, designing sets and costumes for regional theatres including Perth Theatre, Liverpool Playhouse, Royal Lyceum Theatre (Edinburgh), Churchill Theatre (Bromley), Royal Theatre (Northampton). In Northern Ireland he has designed *Noises Off, Arms and the Man* and *The Tempest* (The Lyric Theatre, Belfast); *Cinderella* (The Millennium Forum, Londonderry); and pantomimes for the Ulster Theatre Company. Credits abroad include: *Corpse* and *Ginn Game* (Germany); *Namouna* (Tokyo); *The Natives of Dreamland*, Louisville Ballet (Kentucky); *Melodrame* (New Zealand and South Africa). In the past four years he has designed over 30 productions, many at The Haymarket Theatre in Basingstoke where he is an associate of the artistic team. Credits include *Ghosts, Small Change, Moving Susan, Romeo and Juliet, The Rivals, Pump Boys and Dinettes, Perfect Days, Dracula* and *Jungle Book* (Haymarket Theatre, Basingstoke); *Gypsy* (Guildford School of Acting); *The Bear, I Pagliacci, The Barber of Seville, La Bohème, Cosi fan tutte* and *The Marriage of Figaro* (all for Clonter Opera).

Matt Atwood
Matt Atwood gained a PhD in engineering from Cambridge, before moving into theatre, working as lighting designer, designer, production manager and draughtsman. Over the past five years he has worked with ENO, the Barbican Theatre (London) and the RSC. Design and lighting design credits include: *Bill and Esme* (Chelsea Centre, London); *See How Beautiful I Am* (Pleasance, Edinburgh; Bush Theatre, London); *Bluebeard's Castle* (The Opera Group, Cambridge Corn Exchange); *Eye Contact* (Riverside Studios, London); *Merrily We Roll Along* (Prince's Theatre, London); *Cosi fan tutte* (ADC Theatre, Cambridge); *King's Parade* (Theatre Royal, London); *The Gondoliers* (Minack Theatre, Cornwall).

Neil Austin
Neil Austin studied at the Guildhall School of Music and Drama in London. He went on to be assistant lighting designer to Mark Henderson, before becoming a lighting designer in his own right. He designs mainly for theatre but undertakes architectural and corporate projects as well. Recent theatre credits include: *A Prayer for Owen Meany* (Lyttelton, National Theatre); *The Walls* (Cottesloe, National Theatre); *Further than the Furthest Thing* (Cottesloe and tour); *Japes* (Theatre Royal Haymarket, London); *Trust* (Royal Court, London); *Monkey* (Young Vic, London and tour); *American Buffalo* (Royal Exchange, Manchester); *The Lady in the Van* (West Yorkshire Playhouse); *Al Murray* (Playhouse Theatre, London); *What the Butler Saw* (Theatre Royal, Bath and tour); *Twelfth Night* (Liverpool Playhouse); *The Hairless Diva* and *Full House* (Palace Theatre, Watford); *Loves Work, Cuckoos, Venecia, Marathon* and *Une Tempête* (Gate Theatre, London); *The Liberation of Skopje* and *Leb y Sol* (Riverside Studios, London); *Closer* (Teatro Broadway, Buenos Aires); *Adugna Dance Project* (Street Symphony, Addis Ababa). Musicals include: *Spend! Spend! Spend!* (co-design with Mark Henderson, touring); *My Fair Lady* (Teatro Nacional, Buenos Aires); *Rags* (Guildhall School of Music and Drama); *Cabaret* (MacOwan Theatre, London). Operas include: *The Embalmer* (Almeida Opera, London); *Orfeo* (Opera City, Tokyo and tour of Japan); *Pulse Shadows* (Queen Elizabeth Hall, London) *L'enfant Prodigue, Le Portrait de Manon* and *La Navarraise* (Guildhall School of Music and Drama); *Peter Grimes* (English Touring Opera, Education). Architectural credits: interior and exterior lighting of the *Journey Zone*, Millennium Dome, London (for Imagination).

Avery Associates
Bryan Avery studied architecture at Leicester Polytechnic (now De Montfort University) from 1962 to 1968, followed by an MA in history and theory of architecture at Essex University under Joseph Rykwert and Dalibor Veseley. In 1978, he established Avery Associates, where he brought insights from theoretical studies and research on construction technology into mainstream practice. Martin Pawley, architectural critic, wrote: 'Avery is an example of that rarity among English architects, an innovative thinker. He has the kind of omnivorous grasp of the scope of total architecture that makes him able to transcend the entire discipline from classical aesthetics to high tech engineering'. Over the past 25 years Avery Associates has worked on a wide range of building types and has developed strong connections with the world of the creative arts through projects such as the Museum of the Moving Image, the BFI London IMAX and the Centenary Project for the Royal Academy of Dramatic Art (London). Clients include national institutes, universities, charitable trusts, government organisations and commercial developers. Its work has won many awards and has been written about extensively, both in this country and abroad.

Martyn Bainbridge
Recent theatre designs include: *Brief Encounter* (Lyric Theatre, Shaftesbury Avenue); *Under Milk Wood, The Norman Conquests: Table Manners, Living Together, Round and Round the Garden,* and *Gaslight* (Clwyd Theatr Cymru). Other credits include: *A Little Night Music, The Birthday Party, Kes, My Cousin Rachel, Outside Edge, Pump Boys and Dinettes, Absurd Person Singular, Charley's Aunt, The Shadow of a Gunman, I Have Been Here Before* and the national tour of *Master Forger* (all for Theatre Royal Plymouth); *Measure for Measure* (Nye Theatre, Oslo); *Deathtrap* (Northcott Theatre, Exeter); *Outside Edge* (Churchill Theatre, Bromley); *The Soldier's Tale* (Oxford Playhouse); *On The Razzle* (Leeds Playhouse); *Intimate Exchanges* (Northcott Theatre); *Brief Encounter* (Bill Kenwright Tour). *Opera designs* include: *Beatrice et Benedict* (Indianapolis Opera, USA); *Ariadne auf Naxos* (Garsington Opera); *The Trial* (Collegiate Theatre, London); *Die Zauberflöte* (Kent Opera); *Madama Butterfly* (Phoenix Opera, UK tour); *Norma, La Traviata* (Opera Northern Ireland); *La Rondine* (Royal Academy of Music, London); *Le nozze di Figaro* (Guildhall School of Music and Drama). Ballet designs include: *Daphnis and Chlöe* (The Royal Ballet at the Royal Opera House, Covent Garden and Metropolitan Opera House, New York). Exhibition design credits include: *The Astronomers* (London Planetarium); *Armada 1588-1988* (National Maritime Museum, Greenwich); *Lawrence of Arabia* (National Portrait Gallery, London); *Daendels* (Rijksmuseum, Amsterdam). He also designed a major permanent exhibition for Madame Tussaud's in Amsterdam - *Madam Tussaud Scenerama* - and a new *Chamber of Horrors* (for Madame Tussaud's in London); *Peter the Great* (Queen's House, Greenwich); EMI Centenary Exhibition (London); and *The Explorer's Gallery* (National Maritime Museum).

Simon Banham
Simon Banham has spent the past 20 years designing and devising theatre across Britain. His work has been mainly freelance, but occasionally associated with particular companies, including Contact Theatre, Manchester, where he was head of design (1991-1995); and the performance research company Quarantine, which he joined as a founder member 1999. As a professional designer, he has created over 90 productions, which have taken him throughout Europe and to festivals in Brazil, co-productions in Russia and workshops for students and practitioners in Sierra Leone and India. Since September 1998 he has taught in the Department of Theatre, Film and Television at the University of Wales, Aberystwyth. While there he has been instrumental in establishing a new joint honours programme in scenographic studies. All his work for the university is fed and informed by his continuing career as a freelance designer.

Rob Batterbee
Rob Batterbee trained at Bretton Hall (Leeds University), graduating in 2000. He has skills in all design disciplines and likes to incorporate light and sound into his set and costume designs. Current work is based around small to medium-scale touring, visual and experimental theatre companies. Design work ranges from highly experimental to more conventional formats. A primary concern is the use of space. One exploration of this involved a performance space measuring 3m wide by 45cm deep by 2m tall and involved taut ropes and lots of Lycra!

Ali Bell
Ali Bell initially studied fine art and dance at Roehampton Institute, London, focusing on community art in public spaces, before studying on the post graduate Motley Theatre Design Course (1999-2000). Her designs for theatre include: *A Man for All Seasons* with director, Ester Baker (Young Vic, London); *Accidental Death of an Anarchist* (Synergy Theatre Projects, HMP Wandsworth, London); *Eugene Onegin* (Stag Theatre, Sevenoaks; The White Rock, Hastings); and *Tales of Hoffman*, directed by Orpha Phelan. Film production designs include: *Kiss Me Quick* (Meridian TV's 2001 Taped Up season); the award-winning shorts, *The Return of the Ancient Mariner* and *Shooting Your Own* (Brighton Film Festival and Abbeville Film Festival, France); and several dance-based pieces. Her theatre work has covered many areas, including assistant to Janey Gardiner on *Life on Mars* (Legoland Denmark, USA and Windsor); scenic painting for Told by an Idiot Theatre Company; and costumes for the National Theatre, Holland Park Opera and the RSC at the Roundhouse, London.

Kim Beresford
Kim Beresford took the Motley Theatre Design Course after obtaining a BA Hons in fine art at Wolverhampton Polytechnic. She was a finalist in the Linbury Prize for Stage Design. Theatre includes: *The Lieutenant of Inishmore*, directed by Derek Goldby (Théâtre de Poche, Brussels); Sir Kenneth MacMillan's ballet, *Solitaire* (Noriko Kobayashi Ballet Theatre, Tokyo); *Solitaire* (première at Buxton Opera House and tour, London City Ballet); Handel's *Radamisto*, directed by Robert Chevara (Britten Theatre, Royal College of Music); *Die Entführung aus dem Serail*, directed by Paul Jepson (Theatre Royal, Plymouth, Riverside Studios, Hammersmith and Salisbury Playhouse); *The Lord of the Flies*, directed by Derek Goldby (Théâtre de Poche, Brussels); *Cloud Nine*, directed by Michael Latimer (Lyric Theatre, Hammersmith); *The Silver Tassie*, directed by Charlie Sherman (Drama Centre, London); *Missing*, directed by Derek Goldby (White Bear Theatre, London). Kim Beresford continues to practise as a fine artist.

Janet Bird
Janet Bird trained at Nottingham Trent University (BA) and at Wimbledon School or Art (MA). She works as a freelance set and costume designer for theatre, film and television. Recent theatre credits include: *Wallop Mrs Cox* (Birmingham Repertory Theatre); *A Tale of Two Cities* (Salisbury Playhouse); *Romeo and Juliet* (White Horse Theatre, Germany); *World Goes 'round* (Cabaret Theatre, New York); and *Attempts on her Life* (RADA).

Cecily Kate Borthwick
Trained in theatre design at Wimbledon School of Art, award-winning designer Cecily Kate Borthwick was on the British team for the 1995 Prague Quadrennial. She has designed for French circus company Gosh! (European tour), *Contre Pour* (Barcelona); *Moby Dick* (Walk The Plank – a sea-faring tour); *The Owl and the Pussy Cat* (Bolton Octagon Theatre); *Song of Songs* (Scottish Dance Theatre, Dundee and tour); *No New Miracles* (Boilerhouse); *As you Like It* and *Desperate Journey* (TAG); *Rhinoceros, The Caretaker* and *V* (all as resident designer for the Arches Theatre, Glasgow). She designed extensively for Dundee Rep Dance Company collaborating with New York choreographer David Dorfman and Janet Smith and was co-designer with Steph Hooper, at the Festival Theatre, of the dance piece *La Belle Dame Sans Merci* using Hooper's specifically engineered Rotospere and wheelchairs. Opera and film designs include: *Semele* (director: David McVicar) and *New Arrival*. Site-specific work includes *Arbour*, a promenade dance performance, and *Safe as Houses* (Dogs of Heaven, Manchester). She has worked in schools, using model-making and set design, and is a qualified teacher and practitioner in the healing arts. She is currently illustrating and writing *Mythological Creatures* for Wooden Books. www.co-creator.net.

Will Bowen
Whilst still completing his DPhil in pure mathematics at Oxford University, Will Bowen co-founded the Almeida Theatre in Islington with Pierre Audi and Chris Naylor. At this time he toured extensively with Rowan Atkinson as designer, production and stage manager. He has worked as design co-ordinator on *Phantom of the Opera, Aspects of Love* and *Oliver!* Opera credits include: *Don Pasquale* (Clonter Opera); *La Traviata* (Stowe); *The Rape of Lucretia* (British Youth Opera); *Carmen* (Opera Holland Park, London). Theatre credits include: *Under Milk Wood*; *Helping Harry*. Musicals include: Howard Goodall's *Days of Hope* (Hampstead Theatre, London); *Girlfriends* (Arts Theatre, London); *Romance/Romance* (Gielgud Theatre, London); *The Canterville Ghost* (Northcott Theatre, Exeter). He designed Eddie Izzard's *Definite Article* (on tour) and *One Word Improv.* (Albery Theatre, London) and *The Music of Andrew Lloyd Webber* (Seville, Spain). Designs for theatre spaces include: Sydmonton Court for Andrew Lloyd Webber; Combe Barn for David and Lady Mary Russell; and the National Theatre Lyttleton Transformations Season. He has been theatre consultant for the new Soho Theatre and the National Theatre Olivier environment. He designed Jill Parker's short film *The Girl in the Red Dress*, which was selected for the Cannes Film Festival. His latest work is for a new, musical version of *Peter Pan* for the Royal Festival Hall and Verdi's *Macbeth* for Opera Iceland.

Stephen Brimson Lewis
Stephen Brimson Lewis won the 1994/95 Olivier Award for Best Set Design for *Les Parents Terribles* (National Theatre) which also received the nomination for Best Costumes. Also for the National, he has designed *A Little Night Music, Private Lives* and *Uncle Vanya*.For the RSC he has designed *Timon of Athens, Macbeth, King John* and *Much Ado About Nothing*.On Broadway he received the Tony and Drama Desk Award nominations for Best Set and Best Costumes for *Indiscretions (Les Parents Terribles)* at the Barrymore Theatre. He also designed *Rose* at the Lyceum Theatre. His work in the West End includes: *Mahler's Conversion, Design For Living, Jeffrey Bernard is Unwell*, and *Vanilla*. He has designed for many regional theatres, most recently: *High Society* (Crucible Theatre, Sheffield); *Dreaming* (Royal Exchange Theatre, Manchester), which was nominated for TMA Best Designer Award 1999; *Racing Demon* (Chichester Festival Theatre and Toronto). Opera and ballet designs include: *The Legend of Joseph* (Staatsoper, Berlin), *Tales of Hoffmann* (Sydney Opera House), *The Barber of Seville* (Royal Opera House, London), *Otello* (Vienna State Opera), *The Turn of the Screw* (Australian Opera) and *Dorian Gray* (Monte Carlo Opera). He was production designer for the feature film *Bent* (Film Four International) and *Macbeth* (Illuminations/RSC/Channel Four). He also designed the costumes for *The Nightmare Years* (TNT).

Paul Brown
Paul Brown trained with Margaret Harris at the Riverside Studios and was awarded a Diploma of Honour at the 1999 Prague Quadrennial. He won the Critic's Circle Award in both 2000 and 2001, the Evening Standard Award for Best Design in 2001 and a fellowship of the Welsh College of Music and Drama. Opera credits include: *Falstaff, I Masnadieri, The Midsummer Marriage, Mitridate Re di Ponto* (all Royal Opera, Covent Garden); *King Arthur* (Royal Opera and Le Châtelet, Paris) which won the *Evening Standard* Award for Outstanding Achievement in Opera; *Moses und Aaron, Lady Macbeth of Mtsensk* (Metropolitan Opera, New York); *Parsifal, Peter Grimes* (Opéra de Paris, Bastille); *Rigoletto* (Teatro Real, Madrid); *Fidelio* (ENO); *Pelléas et Mélisande*, and Lulu (Glyndebourne); *L'incoronazione di Poppea* (Teatro Communale di Bologna); *Tom Jones, Zemir et Azor* (Drottningholm Court Theatre, Sweden); *Hamlet and Vanessa* (Opéra de Monte Carlo); *Don Carlos* (Opera Australia, Sydney Opera House). Ballet credits include: *Giselle* (La Scala, Milan).Theatre credits include: *King Lear* and *Platonov* (Almeida Theatre, Kings Cross, London); *The Tempest* (Almeida Theatre); *Coriolanus* and *Richard II* (Almeida Theatre, Gainsborough Studios, London); *Naked* (Almeida and Playhouse); *The Showman* (Almeida); costume credits include: *Medea* (Almeida, Wyndham's Theatre, London and Broadway); *A Lie in the Mind* (Royal Court, London); *Road* (Royal Court Theatre and Lincoln Center, New York). Films have include: *Up at the Villa* and *Angels and Insects* (Oscar nomination).

Terry Brown
Terry Brown trained as a theatre designer at Wimbledon School of Art, graduating in 1969. For most of the next 12 years he worked exclusively in repertory and in theatre in education companies including the Octagon Theatre Bolton, Lincoln Theatre Royal, Manchester Library Theatre, Connaught Theatre, Worthing, Manchester Contact Theatre and M6 Theatre Company. In the early1980s he became freelance and has worked at Bristol Old Vic, the Duke's Lancaster and Manchester Library Theatre. He began to explore other areas, working as an art director with Cosgrove Hall Productions making model animation films for television including *The Wind in the Willows*. He designs for live events, themed exhibitions and parties. The different disciplines cross-fertilise the various facets of his work be they in the theatre or Hampton Court Palace.

Kate Burnett
Kate Burnett is a freelance theatre designer and artist-in-education. Recent design work includes: *Beauty and the Beast* (Library Theatre, Manchester) and five Manchester Arts Education Festivals at the Forum and Contact Theatres. While Head of Design at Contact Theatre, she won the *Manchester Evening News* Award for designs for *The Power of Darkness, To Kill a Mockingbird* and *The Little Prince*. She also won the *Time Out* Award for *Doctor Faustus* (Young Vic, London). Other work has included: *The Little Mermaid* (Sheffield Crucible Studio), *Brighton Rock* (West Yorkshire Playhouse); *Mother Courage* and *The Day After Tomorrow* (National Theatre Education Department); and productions at Birmingham Rep, Liverpool Everyman and Leicester Haymarket. She has designed large-scale performance projects for the Hallé Orchestra, Huddersfield Contemporary Music Festival, BBC Philharmonic and Glyndebourne Education Departments. She recently gained an MA in art and design in education, from the Institute of Education, University of London. She is co-organiser of the *2D>3D* exhibition, catalogue and education programme. She has organised and participated in two previous exhibitions for the Society of British Theatre Designers; *MakeSpace!*, which won the Gold Medal at the 1995 Prague Quadrennial, and *Time+Space* at the Royal College of Art in 1999 and afterwards the Theatre Museum in London. Projects for 2002/3 include: *Oklahoma!* (National Youth Music Theatre) and *Schweyck in the Second World War* (Library Theatre, Manchester).

David Burrows
David Burrows has collaborated with three principal directors over the past 15 years: Phil Young, Alkis Kritikos and David Graham-Young of Contemporary Stage Company (CSC). Work with Phil Young includes: *Crystal Clear* (Wyndhams Theatre, London); *Les Miroirs Brisés* (French Institute, London); *The Train Years* (MOMI, London); *Knickers* (Lyric Theatre Hammersmith, London); *Blood Brothers* (Heilbronn, Germany); and *Tonight: Lola Blau* (Old Red Lion, London). With Alkis Kritikos: *Miss Julie* (Sir Richard Steel Theatre); *The Collector* (Portlands Playhouse, London); the British première of Beckett's *Rough for Theatre 1 & 2* (Theatro Technis, London and tour); *In Other Beasts the Best* (Theatro Technis); *Tartuffe* (National Theatre of Cyprus, Nicosia); *All Cloned Up* by Mike Bennett (touring). Future plans include the British première of Leah Vitali's *Roast Beef* (London, spring 2003, then transferring to Athens as part of the 'Cultural Spring' programme associated with the Olympic Games). Since March 2000, with director David Graham-Young, he has designed three productions for CSC at the Old Red Lion: *A Summer's Day* by Slawomir Mrozek (British première), *Ghosts* and *Mr Paul* by Tankred Dorst (British première). The most recent CSC production was Manuel Puig's *Mystery of the Rose Bouquet* which opened at the Old Red Lion in October 2002. In June 2002 David Burrows was appointed Theatre Programme Area Leader at Wimbledon School of Art (where he trained under Richard Negri), following ten years as course leader of the Technical Arts Interpretation and Design courses. He also led the UK's first MA course in Theatre Design/Scenography from 1989 to 1994. A detailed biography, production photographs, costume designs and press reviews at www.davidburrows.com.

Isabella Bywater
Isabella Bywater trained at the Motley Theatre Design School. Her opera designs include: *The Turn of the Screw*, produced by Robert Carsen; *The Flying Dutchman*, produced by Keith Warner; *The Duenna, La Finta Giardiniera, Madama Butterfly, The Marriage of Figaro, Il Re Pastore, The Elixir of Love, The Emperor of Atlantis, The Dictator, Snegourochka, Ezio* and *La Traviata*, all produced by Stephen Medcalf; *King Arthur*, produced by Francisco Negrin; *Cavalleria Rusticana* and *Pagliacci*, produced by Knut Hendriksen and *The Masked Ball*, produced by Karen Stone. For Jonathan Miller she has designed: *Nabucco* (Zurich Opera); *I Puritani* (Bayerischer Staatsoper, Munich); *Ermione* and *Eugene Onegin* (Santa Fe Opera); and *Don Pasquale* (Maggio Musicale di Firenze). Her plays include: *Titus Andronicus*, directed by Deborah Warner (RSC); *A Midsummer Night's Dream, TheTempest* and *Twelfth Night*, all directed by Deborah Paige; *A Doll's House* and *All My Sons*, directed by David Massarella; *School for Wives*, directed by Lucy Bailey; *Of Mice and Men*, directed by Dominic Cooke and *Hedda Gabler*, directed by Lindy Davies. She is now designing: *Die Entführung aus dem Serail* (Zurich); *Falstaff* (Tokyo) and *L'Elisir d'Amore* (Royal Opera, Stockholm) all produced by Jonathan Miller, and *The Makropulos Case* (Stockholm) produced by Knut Hendriksen.

Nerissa Cargill Thompson
Nerissa Cargill Thompson graduated from Nottingham Trent University in 1995 and works as a freelance designer. She was head of design for Manchester Youth Theatre from 1997-2000, where highlights included the world première of *Airwaves, the Manchester Evening News* Special Award-winning season (1999) and a *Manchester Evening News* nomination

for *Agamemnon* (1998). She has also designed: *Mad Forest*, *The Way of The World*, *Merry Wives of Wigan*, *The Winter's Tale* (Arden School of Theatre); *A Frame of Mind* (Activ8, at Bolton Octagon); *Edward II*, *Light Shining in Buckinghamshire*, *As You Like It* (Salford University Theatre Company) and many fringe productions in Edinburgh, London and Manchester. Work as a scenic artist and prop maker includes shows for the Royal Northern College of Music, Bolton Octagon, Library Theatre, Manchester and Swan Theatre, Worcester. She also teaches workshops in drama, design, masks and puppetry, props and costumes. In 2002 she worked on carnival costumes for Jubilee and Commonwealth parades and as designer on *Ziggurat - The Spiral Way*, the Lowry Centre's Commonwealth Project produced with partner companies Opera North, The Hallé, Birmingham Royal Ballet and Rambert Dance Company.

Alison Chitty
Alison Chitty trained at St Martin's School of Art and at Central School of Art and Design. She won an Arts Council bursary to the Victoria Theatre, Newcastle-under-Lyme, where she was resident designer for seven years and designed over 40 productions. She was resident designer at the National Theatre for eight years, where productions included: *A Month in the Country*, *Don Juan*, *Much Ado About Nothing*, *The Prince of Homburg*, *Danton's Death*, *Major Barbara*, *Kick for Touch*, *Venice Preserv'd*, *Tales From Hollywood*, *Antigone*, *Remembrance of Things Past* (Olivier Award for Best Costume Designer), *Fool for Love*, which transferred to the West End, and *Luther*. She received Olivier Award nominations for *She Stoops To Conquer* and *Martine*. She also designed Sir Peter Hall's productions of *Antony and Cleopatra*, *The Late Shakespeares* (National Theatre) *Orpheus Descending* (Haymarket Theatre, London and Broadway) and *The Rose Tattoo* (The Playhouse, London). Opera credits include: *The Marriage of Figaro* (Opera North, Leeds); *New Year* (Houston Grand Opera and Glyndebourne); *Gawain*, *Arianna*, *The Bartered Bride* (Royal Opera, Covent Garden); *Falstaff* (Gothenburg); *Jenufa* (Dallas); *Billy Budd* (Geneva, Dallas, Houston, Los Angeles, London. Olivier Award, Best Opera Production 1995; Paris: Best Opera Production 1996); *Blonde Eckbert* (Santa Fe); *Khovanshchina* (ENO. Olivier Award, Best Opera Production 1994); *Modern Painters* and *Dialogue des Carmelites* (Santa Fe); *Die Meistersinger* (Copenhagen); *Turandot* (Paris); *Der Fliegender Holländer* (Giulio Cesare (Bordeaux); *Tristan und Isolde* (Chicago and Seattle); *Otello* (Munich); *Aida* (Geneva); *The Last Supper* (Staatsoper Berlin, and Glyndebourne); *La Vestale* (ENO). Recent productions include *Bacchai* (National Theatre and Epidaurus), directed by Sir Peter Hall; *Cavalleria Rusticana* and *I Pagliacci* (Royal Albert Hall) and the Peter Gill Festival in Sheffield. She has designed for several Mike Leigh films: *Life Is Sweet*, *Naked* and *Secrets and Lies*, which won the Palme d'Or at Cannes and was an Academy Award Nominee for Best Picture. Alison Chitty has advised on the design and construction of theatre

buildings in Stoke-on-Trent, Delhi and Johannesburg. She is a lecturer and advisor on theatre design and director of the Motley Theatre Design School.

Bunny Christie
Bunny Christie trained at the Central School of Art in London. She has worked extensively at the National Theatre, most recently designing *A Streetcar Named Desire*, with Glen Close, directed by Trevor Nunn. Her design for *Baby Doll* originated at Birmingham Rep, subsequently moved to the Lyttelton Theatre and then the Albery Theatre in the West End. She won an *Evening Standard* Award for Best Design and an Olivier Award Nomination. Other work at the National Theatre includes: *Dealers Choice* by Patrick Marber and *War and Peace*, a collaboration with Shared Experience. Previous work with Shared Experience was the much acclaimed British and international tour of *Mill on the Floss*, which won a TMA Award for Best Overall Production. She has designed six shows for the Royal Court Theatre (London) winning a *Time Out* Award for *Man to Man* and a London Fringe Award for *The Terrible Voice of Satan*. She has worked on a number of shows for the Tricycle Theatre (London) including *The Colour of Justice*, *The Stephen Lawrence Inquiry*, subsequently filmed by the BBC, and later in the West End. She designed *The Vagina Monologues* in the West End and all-star charity events at the Albert Hall and the Old Vic, raising money for women's charities. She has worked for the Royal Shakespeare Company, the Old Vic, Bristol Old Vic, Shakespeare's Globe, the BBC and on various films. For Renaissance Films, she designed *Swansong*, directed by Kenneth Branagh and starring Sir John Gielgud. This film was nominated for an Academy Award as Best Short Film.

David Cockayne
Designing for performance has always, at best, involved designing for the whole production, conceiving a theatre piece in totality and working in close partnership with the lighting designer. David Cockayne trained as a theatre designer at Birmingham College of Art (1964-67) having previously considered architecture or fine art. He worked at Birmingham Repertory Theatre (Resident Designer 1968-1970), Liverpool Playhouse, Greenwich Theatre, Theatr Clwyd and spent six years as Head of Design at Manchester Library Theatre (1973-1979), including the transfer of *Sell-Out* to the Cottesloe Theatre. Later freelance work has included Greenwich Theatre, the Traverse Theatre, Leeds Playhouse, Leicester Haymarket Studio, Sheffield Crucible, the MAC, Birmingham (*The Wall*, *Satyagraha*, *King*), Duchy Ballet (*Swan Lake*, *Peter and the Wolf*, *Coppelia*) and the Royal Northern College of Music (*Into The Woods*, *The Queen of Spades*). *Tomorrowland* was designed for a production sung in English at the Novaya Opera House in Moscow in 1999. He taught theatre design at Nottingham Trent University, 1980 - 1995. He has given papers at conferences on scenography and education in the UK and overseas. He is now concentrating on design for music theatre, including ballet and returning to the fine art painting, which formed part of the course in theatre design at Birmingham.

Rosemarie Cockayne
Rosemarie Cockayne was born in Montreal and returned to Britain with her family as a young child. She studied ballet with Stanislas Idzikowski and the Royal Ballet Senior School, dancing with Ballet for All. She was Prima Ballerina with the Basle State Ballet and on freelance contracts. She then studied art at Saint Martin's School of Art and Morley College. Her first solo exhibition was at Clarges Gallery, London and since then she has exhibited internationally, while keeping roots in London. Commissions include works on paper, tempera paintings, installation and stage design. Working particularly with the community - the touring multi-media project *Streams of Light* was created with hostels run by Providence Row (men and women street drinkers, cold weather shelters, drop-in centres, hostels for young adults and asylum seekers) - as was the performance-installation *Journey of the Soul*. *River of Life* was designed for the annual service to commemorate those who die homeless. She is very interested in international exchange, education and environment. Recent projects include: *Portraite* with Drapers City Foyer Hostel; and *Bethy and the Plum Tree*, design and ideas for orphaned and abandoned children in China with the Good Rock Foundation Charity UK. She is currently art facilitator at the Pembroke Centre for Mental Health, starting a project on the life of Robert Hooke.

Ken Coker
Ken Coker began his career lighting the Cambridge Footlights and since then has lit work for groups as diverse as the Hank Wangford Band and Rambert Dance Company. As well as pursuing a freelance career, he teaches at the University of Derby on the Live Performance Technology BSc. He is also pursuing an MSc in Multimedia Computing.

David Collis
David Collis originally trained as a potter, then went on to the Motley Theatre Design Course and an Arts Council Design Bursary at the Royal Lyceum Theatre in Edinburgh. He then became head of design at Nottingham Playhouse and subsequently Head of Design at ENO. He now works as a freelance designer.

Sue Condie
Sue Condie trained in theatre design at Middlesex Polytechnic and Nottingham Trent University. For the first four years she worked with a variety of touring companies designing *Tongues Will Wag* for Greenwich YPT; *Can't See The Wood For The Trees* for Roundabout TIE; *Stone Moon* and *T he Party* for Theatr Iolo; and several productions for Action Transport Theatre, including *Macbeth*, *The Magic Book* and *Broken Angel*. She became associate resident designer at the New Victoria Theatre, Newcastle-under-Lyme, where designs have included: *Ghosts*, *Private Lives*, *Oliver Twist*, *The Hound of The Baskervilles*, *Overture*, *Beauty and The Beast*, *Insignificance* and *Aladdin* (costumes) and recently returning to design, *Billy Liar* (also for Stephen Joseph Theatre, Scarborough), *Sweeney Todd* and *Outside Edge*. Other designs include: *East is East*, *Corpse*, *Hot Pants* and *Roughyeds* (Oldham Coliseum);

Insignificance, *Animal Farm*, *Return To The Forbidden Planet* and *Alice* (Harrogate Theatre); *Three Minute Heroes* and *Dick Whittington* (Belgrade Theatre, Coventry); *A Chaste Maid in Cheapside* and *Mother Country* (New Vic, Bristol); and *The Just So Stories*, *Aesop's Fables and Shouting at Shadows* (Sixth Sense Theatre/Cheltenham Everyman). Future projects include: *Twelfth Night* (Cheltenham Everyman) and *Aladdin* (Belgrade Theatre).

Patrick Connellan
Patrick Connellan's theatre credits include: *Edward III* (RSC,Stratford); *Heaven Can Wait* (Belgrade Theatre, Coventry and tour); *Miss Julie* and *The Blue Room* (Octagon Theatre, Bolton); *A Midsummer Night's Dream*, on which he was also associate director (Belgrade Theatre, Coventry); *My Best Friend* (Hampstead Theatre and The Door, Birmingham Rep); *St Joan* (The Door); *The Slight Witch* (National Theatre Springboard and The Door); *Leader of the Pack* (on tour and West End); *A Passionate Woman* (Comedy Theatre, London); *Misery* (Criterion Theatre, London) and *Salad Days* (Vaudeville Theatre, London). He won the Linbury Prize for Stage Design in 1987. In 1989 he designed the indoor production of *Der Fliegende Holländer* for Bregenzer Festspiele. Other theatre includes: *Coriolanus*, *When We Are Married* and *The Rivals* (West Yorkshire Playhouse); *Morning Glory* (The Door, Watford Palace and Cambridge Arts); *Confidence*, *Down Red Lane*, *Rough*, *Pygmalion*, *The Atheist's Tragedy*, *Cider With Rosie*, *The Pied Piper*, *The Grapes of Wrath*, *Nervous Women* and *Julius Caesar* (Birmingham Rep); *Paddy Irishman*, *Paddy Englishman*, *Paddy...* (Birmingham Rep and Tricycle Theatre, London); *The Wizard of Oz* (Leicester Haymarket); *Perfect Days* (Wolsey Theatre, Ipswich and Greenwich Theatre); *A View from The Bridge* (Harrogate Theatre); *A Saint She Ain't* (King's Head Theatre, London); *A Passionate Woman* (Gloria Theatre, Athens); *She Knows You Know* (New Victoria Theatre, Newcastle-under-Lyme); set design for Big Nose (Belgrade Theatre), *Phil and Jill and Jill and Phil* (Swan Theatre, Worcester and Belgrade Theatre); *The Dice House*, *Silas Marner*, *She Stoops To Conquer*, *Leader of the Pack*, *Neville's Island*, *The Wedding*, *Limestone Cowboy* and *The Hound of the Baskervilles* (Belgrade Theatre); *Conduct Unbecoming* (national tour); *Misery* (Leicester Haymarket); *Macbeth*, *Twelfth Night* and *I Have Been Here Before* (Mercury Theatre, Colchester); *Time and the Conways* (Octagon Theatre, Bolton); *Top Girls* (Salisbury Playhouse and The Drum, Plymouth); *The Marriage of Figaro* (New Vic). Patrick Connellan is associate designer at the Belgrade Theatre, Coventry.

Simon Corder
Simon Corder joined the circus as a ringboy when he left school in 1978. He went on to learn his craft as a technician in touring theatre and opera. In 1981 he joined Lumière & Son Theatre Company, lighting theatre shows and site-specific performances in Britain and around the world. As a professional photographer, in the mid 1980s, he combined news and arts photography with original images for projection in performance.

He designed lighting for the first night zoo in the world, *Night Safari Singapore*, which opened in 1996; and the second, in Guangzhou, China. His career as a theatrical lighting designer continues, with over 150 designs for opera, theatre and dance, in situations ranging from Europe's finest opera houses to studios of the avant-garde. He currently enjoys a variety of work including set design, light art installations, collaborations with visual artists, film making, photography, and projection for performance. He also offers production, consultancy and lighting design services to commercial clients.

Charlotte Cridlan
Charlotte Cridlan trained in design at the Bristol Old Vic Theatre School and has a degree in drama and theatre studies from Kent University. Recent designs include: *Tosca, Jago* (world première), *The Beggar's Opera* (Cochrane Theatre, London); *The Ostrich and the Dolphin* (Bloomsbury Theatre, London) for Wedmore Opera; *Pippin* (London Studio Centre); *The Brothers of Brush* (Juno Theatre); *The Watched* (Cornwall) for Bedlam Theatre on tour; theatre in education: *The Tiger of the Seas, Future Perfect* and the world première of *The Empty Chair* (Whitehorse Theatre, Germany); *Travelling Light* (New Vic Basement, Bristol); also in Bristol for Bristol Old Vic Theatre School: *The Front Page* (New Vic Studio, Bristol); *Everyman* (New Vic Basement); and costumes for *Love's Labours Lost* (New Vic Studio). Previous design work on the Edinburgh and London Fringe includes original productions of: *Stealing The Smile* (1998); *Tenth From The End* (1996); and *Our Best Kept Secret* (1996) by Christopher W Hill, productions of *Hysteric Studs* by Charlotte Mann (Edinburgh Festival, 1997; BAC, London, 1998; Theatre Lab, Houston, Texas, 1999. From BOVTS she received the John Elvery Prize for Theatre Design and her design for *Tenth From The End* (Lumley Studio, Canterbury, 1996) was 'highly commended' by the National Student Drama Festival. Other design work in Canterbury includes: *Cinnamon's Splinter* by Carl Grose (Gulbenkian Theatre) and a double bill of *After Magritte* and *Ashes and Sand* (Lumley Studio). She has worked as an assistant designer on short films for HTV Bristol and Brownian Motion Pictures and also as a scenic artist in Bristol for Stage Electrics, The Redgrave Theatre and BOVTS.

Judith Croft
Judith Croft's first degree was in fashion textiles, then she studied theatre design at the Bristol Old Vic Theatre School. She was resident designer at the Gateway Theatre, Chester, then head of design at the Oldham Coliseum before going freelance in 1986. She became head of design at the Library Theatre, Manchester in 1991 and continues to work there on a regular basis. For the Library Theatre, she has designed many successful productions of plays by Neil Simon including *The Brighton Beach Trilogy* and *Laughter on the 23rd Floor*, which she also designed for the West End run, starring Gene Wilder. She has designed several musicals, working with director Roger Haines, including *Assassins, Goodnight Mr Tom* and *Company*. She designed the last two rock 'n' roll

musicals for Theatr Clwyd, written and directed by Peter Rowe. She designed *Falstaff* for the Royal Northern College of Music, winning the *Manchester Evening News* Award for Best Production of an Opera (2001). She designed *The Borrowers*, which started at the Library Theatre and has now completed two national tours. Recent work for the Library Theatre includes: *Pygmalion* with Chris Honer and *The Memory of Water* with Roger Haines.

Sean Crowley
Sean Crowley trained at Wimbledon School of Art, graduating in 1985 with first class honours. After an early career as an assistant to many of Europe's leading designers, with companies such as the Royal Opera, the Metropolitan Opera and the RSC, and as a designer for theatre ranging a one-person cabaret to community operas with a cast of 300, he returned to Wales to live and work. He has designed over 70 productions in Wales since 1995, making only brief excursions to the Soho Theatre, London, in collaboration with Script Cymru, the Hampstead Theatre, London, the Sherman Theatre, Cardiff and the Danish Royal Opera. He was appointed design lecturer at the Welsh College of Music and Drama in 1998 and since 1999 he has been the head of design. He is currently the British Design Schools exhibition organiser for PQ'03 and is a member of the Linbury Biennial committee.

Gabriella Csanyi-Wills
Gabriella Csanyi-Wills, Hungarian by parentage, British by birth, and French by education, has a degree in humanities from the Open University and a degree in theatre studies from Central School of Speech and Drama. Since finishing her studies in 1996, she has worked consistently, designing set and costumes for theatre, opera and dance. She is involved with educational programmes and workshops such as Pan Arts week of work and play with dancers, musicians and poets, to understand the processes through which each of us go to arrive at the finished work, creating greater collaboration and a huge amount of fun. Her recent theatre credits include: *Die Fledermaus* (Robert Bouffler Trust); *Blazing 2000* (Royal Festival Hall, London); *Beauty and the Beast* (West Sussex Youth Theatre); *The Merry Widow* (Opera della Luna); *Julius Caesar Jones* (Music Box); *16 Winters* (Bristol Old Vic); *Jump to Cow Heaven* (Wimbledon Studio); *Henry V* and *Falstaff* (Queen Elizabeth's Hospital School, Bristol); *Livid* (Australia and England tour); *Chair Lift* (Hampstead Theatre, London); *Jessie* (RSC Summerhouse and Edinburgh Fringe); *The Member of the Wedding* (Wimbledon Studio); *The Lodger* (Jermyn Street Theatre, London); *Refract* (The Place, London and tour); *A Midsummer Night's Dream* and *Hamlet* (Cannizaro Park, London).

Anne Curry
Anne Curry has a degree in theatre design and has completed two years post graduate study at the Slade School of Art. She received the Sir Barry Jackson Memorial Scholarship and the Jacobs Memorial Award, and worked in Rome, Florence and Vienna after receiving a travel bursary from the Royal Society of Arts. A wide variety of design experience includes both

resident and freelance work. She worked at Oldham Coliseum after receiving an Arts Council design bursary. *Dreams of San Francisco*, (Bush Theatre, London) won the Thames Television Award for Best Production (1978); *The Boys in the Band* (King's Head and Aldwych Theatres, London, 1997); The Vivian Ellis Prize (Her Majesty's Theatre, London, 1997). Previous design work was submitted as part of the British entry in the 1999 Prague Quadrennial. She joined the department of theatre design at Nottingham Trent University in January 2002, as senior lecturer in costume design and interpretation. Prior to that she was course director of the BA (Hons) Theatre Design, BA (Hons) Performance Design and MA Scenography at the University of Central England. She is completing an MA in education and has been a visiting tutor at Central School of Speech and Drama. Nine recent designs for the Birmingham Theatre School include the Shakespeare in Education tour and *Oh, What A Lovely War!* (Social History Gallery, Birmingham Museum and Art Gallery).

Ann Curtis
Ann Curtis trained at Central St Martin's College of Art and Design. She spent three seasons as Ladies' Cutter at the Royal Shakespeare Theatre followed by several seasons collaborating with John Bury on costumes for: *The Wars of the Roses, The Histories Cycle, Hamlet* and *Indians*. Other productions at the RST included: *The Government Inspector, The Tempest, The Romans Season* and sets and costumes for *Theatre Go Round*. Other costume designs include: *Moses und Aron, Die Zauberflöte* (also with John Bury); *Troilus and Cressida* (Royal Opera, Covent Garden); *A Night in Venice, Don Carlos* (ENO); *Owen Wingrave* (Glyndebourne); *A Midsummer Night's Dream* (Copenhagen); *The Merchant, St Joan, The Beggar's Opera* (Birmingham Rep); *Uncle Vanya, Man and Superman* (Haymarket, London); *Me and My Girl* (Leicester Haymarket; Adelphi, London, and Broadway) which received New York Tony and Drama Desk Award nominations. Since 1980 she has worked mainly in Canada at the Stratford Festival (including some set design), in London, Ontario; in Edmonton, Alberta; for the Canadian Opera Company in Toronto and on a film, *The Wars*. New York productions include *Jekyll and Hyde*, which was nominated for a Tony. She has taught the history of costume and costume design at Central Saint Martin's in London, at the Montreal Theatre School and currently at the Motley School of Theatre Design in London.

Charles Cusick-Smith
Charles Cusick-Smith was born in Glasgow. He studied first at Glasgow School of Art and then at the Slade School of Art in London. In 1981 he was seconded to English National Ballet as an Arts Council trainee designer. From 1982-86 he was associate designer with the Library Theatre, Manchester. Since 1986 he has been working freelance for most of the theatres in Britain, designing dramas, musicals and pantomimes. Musical credits include: the European premieres of Sondheim's *Follies* and *Pacific Overtures, West Side Story, Company, Beehive, Hold Tight It's 60s Night*; co-designer of *Hot Stuff* and

Heavenly Bodies; A Slice of Saturday Night with Barbara Dickson and the latest musical-biography of Dusty Springfield, *Dusty*, starring Mari Wilson; *Edward II*, starring Eddie Izzard; costumes for *Something Else* (Boyzone tour 1997); *Rock Around The Dock* (Granada TV); stage design for the International Windmill Club; Most recently, he designed *The Guardsman* starring Greta Scacchi. In 1996 he began to design opera and ballet productions abroad: *The Wall, Nabucco, Otello, Aida* and *Don Carlos* (Germany); *Romeo and Juliet* and *The Nutcracker* (Estonian National Opera); *Il Trovatore* (Grand Theatre, Cultural Centre, Hong Kong). Forthcoming productions include: *Cat on a Hot Tin Roof* (UK) and *Der Rosenkavalier* (Germany). He received a *Manchester Evening News* Award for Best Designer (1986) and the TMA Award for Best Design for *The Plough and the Stars* (1993).

Es Devlin
Es Devlin trained at Bristol University, Central Saint Martin's and Motley Theatre Design Course. Theatre designs include: *Howie the Rookie* (Bush Theatre, London. TMA Award for Best Design 1999); *Meat* (Plymouth Theatre Royal. Nominated for TMA Best Design 2001); *Antony and Cleopatra, Henry IV, The Prisoner's Dilemma* (RSC); *Betrayal* (National Theatre); *Hinterland* (National Theatre/Out of Joint); *Rita, Sue and Bob Too, A State Affair* (Out of Joint); *Hamlet* (Young Vic, London); *Credible Witness* (Royal Court, London); *Yard Gal* (Royal Court); *Snake in the Grass* (Old Vic, London); *Piano* (TPT, Tokyo); *Love and Understanding, Love You Too, One Life and Counting, Drink, Dance, Laugh, Lie* (all Bush Theatre, London); *Perapalas* (Gate Theatre, London); *The Death of Cool* (Hampstead Theatre, London); *Closer to Heaven* (Arts Theatre, London); *A Day in the Death of Joe Egg* (Ambassadors, London); *Arabian Night* (Actors Touring Company); *That Was Then* (Abbey Theatre, Dublin); *Edward II* (Octagon Theatre, Bolton. Linbury Prize for Stage Design, 1995). Opera designs include: *Macbeth* (Klangbogen, Vienna); *Powder Her Face* (Ystad Festival, Sweden); *Hansel and Gretel* (Scottish Opera Go Round); *Fidelio* (English Touring Opera). Designs for dance include: *A Streetcar Named Desire* (Northern Ballet Theatre); *God's Plenty* (Rambert Dance Company); *Four Scenes* (Rambert); *New Work* (Cullberg Ballet, Sweden). Designs for film include: *Victoria Station; Brilliant!* (BBC2); *Snow on Saturday; A Tale of Two Heads; Beggars Belief*.

Robin Don
Robin Don studied art and engineering in Edinburgh before working with designer Ralph Koltai. Since gaining a sturdy theatrical grounding with this top designer, he has designed productions in many countries around the world. In 1996, he was named 'Designer of the Year', by London's Critic's Circle for his designs for Sharman MacDonald's *The Winter Guest* (Almeida Theatre, London) and was production designer for the film of *The Winter Guest*, directed by Alan Rickman, which was highly praised at the Venice Film Festival. Theatre designs include: *When I Was A Girl I Used To Scream and Shout, Kiss of the Spiderwoman, The Marshalling Yard,*

Beautiful Thing (Bush Theatre, London); *The Ticket of Leave Man* (National Theatre); *Twelfth Night, Les Enfants du Paradis* (RSC); *A Walk in the Woods*, with Sir Alec Guiness (Comedy Theatre, London); *Fool for Love* (Donmar Warehouse, London). Opera and ballet designs include: *Carmen* (Lyric Opera of Chicago); *Peter Grimes, The Force of Destiny* (Sydney Opera House); *The Midsummer Marriage, Eugene Onegin* (San Francisco Opera); *Don Quichotte* (New York City Opera); *Tamerlano* (Opéra de Lyon); *A Midsummer Night's Dream, Norma* (Royal Opera, Covent Garden); *Turandot*, the ballet (Guangzhou City Ballet China). Musicals include: Andrew Lloyd Webber's *Song and Dance* (Palace Theatre, Watford); *Ziegfeld* (London Palladium); *The Boy Friend* (Old Vic, London); The Rocky Horror Show (Piccadilly Theatre and national tours). In 1979 his design for *Eugene Onegin* at the Aldeburgh Festival, conducted by Rostropovich) was part of the British entry at the 1979 Prague Quadrennial, which won the Golden Troika.

Minty Donald

Minty Donald studied theatre and art history at the University of Glasgow and trained in theatre design at Glasgow School of Art. After a season at the Library Theatre in Manchester, she returned to Scotland to freelance, focusing on small-scale, touring, community and devised work. She has designed for many of the country's leading theatre, dance and performance companies including: The Traverse Theatre, Edinburgh; 7:84 Theatre Co, Scotland; Suspect Culture, Glasgow; TAG Theatre Co, Glasgow; Dundee Rep; CCA, Glasgow; Edinburgh International Festival; Royal Scottish National Orchestra and Scottish Ballet. Throughout the UK she has worked for, among others, WSI International and London Contemporary Dance. Recent theatre and performance includes: *Marching On, A Little Rain, Under Construction, Whispers of Water and Yarns* (7:84); *Red,* (Catherine Wheels Theatre Company); *Love Songs in a Lonely Desert Full of Crying Men and Howling Women* (Anatomy Performance Company); *Home* (Look Out Theatre Company); and *The Bay* (EGYT/Tron Theatre). Minty Donald is currently exploring the use of digital imaging technologies as a means of generating design-led performance. She lectures in scenography and theatre space at the University of Glasgow.

Keith Dunne

Keith Dunne trained in theatre design and graduated in 2000 from Central Saint Martin's College of Art and Design after a career of ten years in the Royal Navy. He recently toured with the award-winning play *Splendour* for Paines Plough. His theatre design credits include: *Pinocchio* (Chicken Shed Theatre Company, London); *All for Love* (BAC, London); *Sentence Deferred, Mother's Boy* and *Fred & Ginger* (Rosemary Branch Theatre, London); and *Cat on a Hot Tin Roof* (Ohio University). Opera designs include: *The Merry Widow* (Colombia Artist, tour USA 2001-2002); *Die Fledermaus* (Société Anonyme de Représentation Artistique); *Rigoletto* (Malvern Theatre Festival); *La Traviata* (Surrey Opera); *Suor Angelica and Pulcinella* (Abbey Opera). Musical credits include: *Company* (Tower

Theatre, London) and *Cabaret* (Millfield Theatre, London). For television: *Footballers' Wives* (ITV, Shed Productions). He is currently working on a new series of *Silent Witness* (BBC) and *Madam Butterfly* (Colombia Artist, touring USA 2002-2003).

Alex Eales

Alex Eales trained at Wimbledon School of Art, London. He was resident designer at E15 Acting School in 2000. Before and since then, he has been working freelance. During the past few years he has designed almost exclusively on new writing projects for rural touring companies and, rather bizarrely, shows in Milton Keynes. He designed *The Tractor Girls* for Oxfordshire Touring Theatre Company and *The Walsingham Organ* for Eastern Angles Theatre Company, both of which toured and went to the Pride of Place Festival in Salisbury in 2002. He has designed over 40 shows in the past five years, working in Aberdeen, Edinburgh, Cambridge, Oxford, Salisbury, Watford, London and Los Angeles among other cities. Currently he lives and works in a small village in Bedfordshire. Pictures and more information from www.alexeales. co.uk.

Paul Edwards

Paul Edwards was born in Australia and studied at the Royal Academy of Dramatic Art, graduating with honours. Theatre design credits include: *Little Women* (Sheffield Crucible); *The Last Yankee* (Leicester Haymarket); *The Importance of Being Earnest, Cat on a Hot Tin Roof, Private Lives, The Odd Couple, On the Piste, Gasping, Romeo and Juliet* (Harrogate Theatre); *Vita and Virginia* (Sphinx Theatre Company); *The Young Idea* (Chester Gateway); *Noises Off, Great Expectations, The Sound of Music, The Turn of the Screw, Dames at Sea* (Queen's Theatre, Hornchurch); *The Servant of Two Masters* (Wolsey Theatre, Ipswich); *Threesome, Stupid Cupid, F***ing Martin* (Sweatshop Theatre Company); *Fair Game* (Theatre Royal, Plymouth); *Kiss Me Kate* (Norwich Playhouse); *Brighton Beach Memories*, costumes (Stephen Joseph Theatre Scarborough); *Pygmalion, Hamlet, The Seagull, School for Scandal* (Theatr Clwyd); *The Importance of Being Earnest* (National Theatre of Israel); *No Flies on Mr. Hunter* (Chelsea Arts Theatre, London); *The Pleasure Principle* (Young Vic, London); *Viva Espana* (Arts Theatre, London); *The Taming of the Shrew* (Regent's Park Open Air Theatre, London); *Is That All There Is?,* costumes (Almeida, London and New York); *Trelawny of the Wells* (West End); *Jyro-Scape, Boutique* (Sadler's Wells, London). Designs for opera include: *The Bartered Bride, Orfeo ed Euridice, Die Zauberflöte*, costumes (The New Israeli Opera, Tel Aviv); *The Mikado* (Sherman Theatre, Cardiff); *L'Egoiste* (Royal Academy of Music, London); *Il Mondo della Luna, L'Italiana in Algieri* (Garsington Opera); *Der Jakobin* (Wexford Festival Opera); *Orfeo ed Euridice* (Opéra National du Rhin, Strasbourg and Teatro Calderon); *The Marriage of Figaro* (Opera Ireland); *La Finta Semplice* (Opéra de Nice and L'Opéra Comique, Paris); *Die Walküre* (Teatro Teresa Carreno, Caracas); *Il Matrimonio Segreto* (L'Opéra Comique, Paris).

Lis Evans

Lis Evans trained at Cardiff Art College and Trent Polytechnic, graduating in 1987. She went on to design, paint and make props for various productions, exhibitions and trade shows, including Circus Senso's *Christmas Show* (Hackney Empire, London) and *Equus* (Incompany Theatre). As resident designer at the New Vic Theatre in Staffordshire since 1991, she has designed over 40 productions, including: *Sweeney Todd, Kiss of the Spiderwoman, Translations, The Cherry Orchard, The Tempest, Carmen, From a Jack to a King, Twelfth Night, The Hunchback of Notre Dame, A Comedy of Errors, The Wizard of Oz, The Mikado, Top Girls, The Magic Flute, Pat and Margaret, The Snow Queen, Cleo, Camping, Emanuelle and Dick, Toad of Toad Hall, The Railway Children, Hamlet, Ali Baba, My Mother Said, Talking Heads* (also in Liverpool and Harrogate) and. most recently, *The Beauty Queen of Leenane.* She has recently returned to the New Vic as head of design, after having her third daughter, to design the *Snow Queen* for Christmas 2002.

David Farley

David Farley graduated from Wimbledon School of Art in 1999. Recent design work includes: *Observe the Sons of Ulster Marching Towards the Somme*, directed by James Philips (Jericho Productions, The Pleasance, London); *The Seagull,* directed by Simon Godwin (Royal Theatre, Northampton); *Dealer's Choice*, directed by Angus Jackson (Clwyd Theatr Cymru); *Sexual Perversity in Chicago* and *The Shawl*, directed by Angus Jackson (Crucible Theatre, Sheffield); *Pink Orthodox* (Shunt, Riverside Studios, London); *Works on Canvas* and *Here Lie Hedwig and Stoller* (Shunt, The Arch, Bethnal Green, London); *The Dybbuk* directed by Mark Rosenblatt - production awarded the James Menzies-Kitchen Memorial Trust Award (BAC, London); *Someone Who'll Watch Over Me* directed by Mark Rosenblatt (Burton-Taylor Theatre, Oxford); *Taming of the Shrew* and *Macbeth* (OUDS Japan Tour - Tokyo Globe and Osaka Maytheatre).

Paul Farnsworth

Paul Farnsworth trained in theatre design at Wimbledon School of Art. He was resident designer for a season at Chichester's new Minerva studio. Other designs at the Chichester Festival Theatre include: *The Pied Piper of Hamelin, The Wind In The Willows, Point Valaine, Valentine's Day, The Power and the Glory, 70 Girls 70.*Several of these also transferred to the West End, where he has designed ; *The Cherry Orchard,* directed by Sam Mendes (Aldwych Theatre); *Moby Dick - a Whale of a Tale* (Picadilly Theatre); *Edna the Spectacle* (Theatre Royal Haymarket); and Sondheim's musical *Passion* (Queen's Theatre. European premiere). Elsewhere: *Privates on Parade* (Greenwich Theatre); *Huis Clos* (Lyric Theatre, Hammersmith); *The Fantasticks, The Merry Wives of Windsor, A Funny Thing Happened on The Way To The Forum, Lady Be Good, A Midsummer Night's Dream, A Connecticut Yankee, The Music Man, Paint Your Wagon, Kiss Me Kate, Troilus and Cressida* and *Gentlemen Prefer Blondes* (Regent's Park); *The Pirates of Penzance* (West Yorkshire Playhouse); *Peter Pan* (Theatr Clwyd);

My Father's House (Birmingham Rep); *Salt of The Earth, Teechers, Hedda Gabler, The Rocky Horror Show, Calamity Jane, Sweeney Todd, Aladdin, A Woman of No Importance, Into The Woods* (Leicester Haymarket); *Good Morning Bill, The Card, Thark* (Watermill Theatre); *Mrs Warren's Profession* (Yvonne Arnaud, Guildford); *Same Old Moon, Little Foxes, Rough Crossing, The Taming of The Shrew, On The Razzle, Keyboard Skills, The Comedy of Errors* (Nuffield Theatre, Southampton); *Volpone* and *The Merchant of Venice* (English Shakespeare Company); *Scrooge* (UK andAustralian tours); *Hayfever, A Flea in Her Ear, Sleuth, My Fair Lady, Peter Pan* (Det Ny Theater, Copenhagen). Recent work includes:*Sleuth, A Saint She Ain't* (Apollo Theatre); *On Your Toes, A Little Night Music, The Crucible* (Leicester Haymarket); *Whistle Down The Wind* (UK tour); *Wind In The Willows* (Birmingham Rep); *Ghosts* (Comedy Theatre, London); *Dorian* (Theatre Royal Windsor); *The Lady In The Van* (Birmingham Rep); *Fallen Angels* (Apollo Theatre and tour); and *Warwickshire Testimony* (RSC); *Follies* (Royal Festival Hall, London). Paul was nominated for a 1997 Olivier Award for his set design of *Passion.*

Rick Fisher

Originally from the US, Rick Fisher has worked in British theatre for over 20 years and is currently chairman of the Association of Lighting Designers. He won the 1998 Olivier Award for his lighting of *Lady in the Dark* and *Chips with Everything* at the National Theatre. He participated in the 1995 Prague Quadrennial with Ian MacNeil, showing *An Inspector Calls* (Tony, Drama Desk awards for the Broadway production; Ovation and Critics' Circle awards for the Los Angeles production) and *Machinal* (Olivier Award 1994). He was at the 1999 Prague Quadrennial with Adventure in Motion Pictures' *Swan Lake.*

Anna Fleischle

Anna Fleischle was born in 1971 in Munich, Germany. She studied theatre design at Central Saint Martin's College of Art and Design in London. Her work as a designer at Theater Erlangen, Germany immediately after her degree, gave her instant recognition, resulting in various productions for the Badisches Staatstheater (National Theater Baden), where she worked with company director Olaf Schmidt. Now based in London, she works for theatres throughout Europe. She designs set and costumes for drama, dance and opera but also develops concepts with directors, choreographers and writers. Her most recent productions include designs for Sadler's Wells and the Royal Ballet.

Richard Foxton

Richard Foxton trained at Trent Polytechnic, Nottingham. His freelance work includes: *Big Night Out at the Palace Theatre* and *Cor! Blimey* (Palace Theatre, Watford); *Hector's House* and *The Importance of Being Earnest* (Lipservice on tour); *Things We Do For Love* and *Death of a Salesman* (Library Theatre, Manchester); *Macbeth, The Miser, Equus, Dead Funny* and *Noises Off* (Salisbury Playhouse); *Double Indemnity, A Family Affair* and *It's a Mad World, My Masters* (New Wolsey Theatre, Ipswich); *Kvetch* (West

Yorkshire Playhouse); *The Firebird* (The Duke's, Lancaster); *Kes, the Musical* (Theatre Royal, York); *A Clockwork Orange* (TAG on tour); *Oedipus Tyrannos* (Contact Theatre, Manchester); *Murderer Hope of Womankind* (Whitworth Art Gallery. Manchester). The latter was part of the gold medal-winning British entry to the 1995 Prague Quadrennial. Richard was resident designer at the Octagon Theatre, Bolton between 1993 and 1999, designing over 40 productions, including: *A Skull in Connemara, Woman in Mind, Neville's Island, Blithe Spirit, Saved, Hysteria, Enjoy, Dancing at Lughnasa, Macbeth, A Midsummer Night's Dream, Blood Wedding, Under Milk Wood, Happy Days, The Fastest Clock in the Universe* and *The Pitchfork Disney*. He has won four *Manchester Evening News* Design Awards in 1992, 1994, 1999 and 2000. In 1997 he was a judge of the Linbury Prize.

Arnim Friess
Arnim Friess initially trained as a photographer. After receiving an MA in scenography at Birmingham Institute of Art and Design, he specialised in designing dynamic performance environments, blending different media such as slide and video projection, lighting and sculptural set-objects. At the heart of each project lies filming, photographing and designing material specifically for use in a three-dimensional space. His work has been seen in the UK, Germany, Italy, Canada, the USA and Denmark. Credits include: *Bricks-in-space Spectacle Life on Mars* (Legolands worldwide); the appearance of hundreds of angels inside St Paul's Cathedral (City of London Festival); *My Beautiful Laundrette* (Snap Theatre); *Angels in America* (Sheffield Crucible); the award-winning *Rumblefish* and *Lord of the Flies* (Pilot Theatre) *Oliver* (Liverpool Playhouse); Mozart's *Mass in C-minor* (Birmingham Royal Ballet); *The Wall* and *Satyagraha* (Midlands Arts Centre), *Shot Through the Heart* (Pentabus Theatre); *Metropolis* and *The Importance of Being Earnest* (Kaos Theatre); *City of Angels* (Guildford School of Acting) and *Hard Day's Night* (Hull Truck Theatre Company). Other work includes exhibition design, lighting an MTV video for trash metal stars Cradle of Filth and a 360-degree, AV installation at The Republic (Sheffield). He also works as a photographer and graphic designer.See www.arnim.co.uk.

Gemma Fripp
After graduating in theatre design (First Class) from Wimbledon School of Art, Gemma Fripp was a 1995 finalist for the Linbury Prize for Stage Design. Her varied work in theatre, musicals and opera has been seen in London's West End and both nationally and internationally. Recent theatre credits include: *Fen* and *Sharp Relief* (Salisbury Playhouse); *Hard Times* (Theatre Royal Haymarket, London); *The Merchant of Venice* and *Don Juan Comes Back From the War* (Lyric Studio, Hammersmith); *A Christmas Carol* (Wolsey Theatre, Ipswich); and *Abigail's Party* (Nuffield Theatre, Southampton). Forthcoming productions: *The Taming of the Shrew* (Salisbury Playhouse); *Dead Wait* and *On My Birthday* (Royal Exchange Studio, Manchester); *As You Like It* (Sphinx Theatre Company). Opera credits include: *Toreador* (Batignano Festival); *Il Re Pastore* (Linbury Studio, London and tour); *Dialogues des Carmelites* (Festival Theatre, Edinburgh) and co-designer on *Cosi fan tutte* (Grange Park Opera).

Soutra Gilmour
Soutra Gilmour graduated from Wimbledon School of Art with first class honours. She has since done a wide variety of design work in theatre, opera and film. Theatre credits include: *Peter Pan* (The Tramway, Glasgow); *Antigone* (Citizens Theatre, Glasgow); *Macbeth* and *Romeo and Juliet* (English Shakespeare Company touring) *Cinderella* and *Hansel and Gretel* (Unicorn Theatre, The Arts); *My Mother Said I Never Should* (Derby Playhouse); *Forty Years On, Real Inspector Hound* and *Black Comedy* (Northcott Theatre, Exeter); *Fool for Love* (English Touring Theatre); *The Birthday Party* (Sheffield Crucible); *Hand in Hand* (Hampstead Theatre); *The Winter's Tale, The Woman Who Swallowed a Pin* (Southwark Playhouse, London); *Sun is Shining* (King's Head, London); *Tear from a Glass Eye, Les Justes, Box of Bananas, Ion* and *Witness* (The Gate, London); *The Shadow of a Boy* (National Theatre). Opera includes: *La Bohème* (Opera Ireland touring); *Eight Songs for a Mad King* (world tour); *El Cimarron* (Queen Elizabeth Hall, London); *Bathtime* (ENO Studio, London); *Twice Through the Heart* (Lowry Centre, Salford); *A Better Place* (ENO, London). Films include: *Amazing Grace* (Parallax Films, C4), *Silent Grace* (Irish Screen).

Roger Glossop
Roger Glossop started his career at Sheffield's Crucible Theatre. He designs regularly for Alan Ayckbourn: at Scarborough, in the West End, at the National Theatre and the RSC. Designs have included: *The Norman Conquests, Woman in Mind, Wildest Dreams, Communicating Doors* (also Chicago); *'Tis Pity She's a Whore, Henceforward..., Comic Potential, Things We Do For Love; House & Garden, Damsel in Distress, Snake in the Grass, Joking Apart, By Jeeves* (Scarborough, London, Connecticut, Los Angeles, Washington and recently filmed by CBC Toronto). Other London credits include: *Mandragola, Rosmersholme* (also New York), *Indigo, Chicago, Annie Get Your Gun* and *Arturo Ui*. Work abroad includes: *The Caretaker* (Berlin); *Sweeney Todd* (Tel Aviv); *Glengarry Glenross* (Brussels). He is director and designer of two award-winning attractions: The World of Beatrix Potter in the Lake District and The Wind in the Willows in Rowsley, Derbyshire. He is a director of the Bowness Theatre Festival and the Old Laundry Theatre, Bowness, which opened in 1992 primarily for the transfer of Alan Ayckbourn's Scarborough productions and around which the annual festival has developed.

Michael E Hall
Michael Hall first became involved in theatre whilst studying for an engineering degree. Work at the Glasgow Citizens and the Half Moon, in London, led to his interest in lighting. His first designs were *Kiss of the Spiderwoman, Romeo and Juliet* (York Theatre Royal); *'Tis Pity She's a Whore, Bring Down The Sun* (The Duke's, Lancaster) and promenade productions of *The Tempest, Much Ado About Nothing, The Wind in the Willows* and *The Tales of King Arthur*. He has lit many productions for Cheltenham Everyman including: *The Mayor of Casterbridge, The Pickwick Papers, Amadeus, Annie, Death and the Maiden, The Sound of Music, Little Shop of Horrors* and two productions of *Macbeth*. The designs for the 1992 production formed a part of the British gold medal-winning entry to the 1995 Prague Quadrennial. Other work includes: *Hamlet* (Kaos Theatre Company); *She Knows You Know* (West Yorkshire Playhouse); *Two Way Mirror, Brother Eichmann* (Library Theatre, Manchester); *La Bohème* (English Touring Opera); *King Lear* (Cork Opera House); *My Cousin Rachel* (Derby Playhouse); *Last of the Red Hot Lovers, Gaslight* (Bolton Octagon); *Second From Last in The Sackrace* (Harrogate Theatre); *Love of the Shelf* (Nuffield Theatre, Southampton); *Scary Antics, Fallen Angels* (Shysters Theatre Company); *A Midsummer Night's Dream* (Belgrade Theatre, Coventry); *The Libertine* (Central School of Speech and Drama, London); *Into The Woods* (Royal Northern College of Music); *Flavio* (Handel Society at The Royal College of Music) and *The Sound of a Hammer* (New Theatre Works). He has also lit exhibitions for the Theatre Museum, including *Let Paul Robeson Sing* and exhibitions about Rambert and Theatre de Complicité.

Peter Ruthven Hall
Peter Ruthven Hall originally trained as an architect. He now works as a stage designer and theatre consultant.
He has worked extensively in opera, in the UK and elsewhere in Europe. Productions range from repertory works to rare operas, many of them premiere performances: *The Turn of the Screw* (Snape Maltings), *Flavio* and *Ottone* (London Handel Festival), *Jenufa, Le nozze di Figaro, La Bohème, Albert Herring* and *Roberto Devereux* (Royal Northern College of Music); *L'Arlesiana* (Opera Holland Park, London); *Lakmé* (Opera Ireland); Mendelssohn's *Camacho's Wedding* and Schubert's *Fierrabras* (Oxford Playhouse); and costume designs for *Tosca* (Malmö Musikteater); *Madama Butterfly* (Royal Danish Opera); *The Turn of the Screw* (Opera Northern Ireland); *Zar und Zimmermann* (Stadttheater Aachen); *Don Giovanni* and *Die Zauberflöte* (Vienna Kammeroper). In musical theatre he has designed original workshop productions of Andrew Lloyd Webber's *Sunset Boulevard* (Sydmonton Festival); *Tutankhamun* (Imagination) and *World Café* (Edinburgh Festival); and in theatre: *Love! Valour! Compassion!* (European première - Library Theatre, Manchester), *Long Day's Journey into Night* (Theatre Royal, Plymouth & Young Vic, London), *The Grapes of Wrath* (Crucible Theatre, Sheffield); *Women of Troy* and *Vassa Zheleznova* (Gate Theatre, London) and *The House of Bernarda Alba* (Oxford Playhouse). For the international design group, Imagination, his work has included the sets for *Joy to the World* at the Royal Albert Hall (in four consecutive years) broadcast on BBC1. He was one of the award-winning British designers exhibiting at the 1995 international Prague Quadrennial exhibition of stage design.
He is secretary of the Society of British Theatre Designers and co-organiser of *2D>3D* and of previous exhibitions: *Make SPACE!* and *Time + Space*.

Abigail Hammond
Abigail Hammond graduated from the Laban Centre London in 1985 with a BA Hons in dance theatre.
Having majored in design, she then went on to work in the college's design department for two years before becoming freelance. In 1989 she set up her own company, Mele of London, producing theatre costumes, exclusive fashion and millinery collections, educational props and costumes and commercial promotional wear. As a designer, her work has been predominantly in dance and she has worked with over 80 choreographers, creating designs for a variety of dance styles and productions. For 12 years the resident designer for the National Youth Dance Company, she is currently resident designer with Union Dance Company, whose work is concerned with reflecting the growing cultural fusion of contemporary society. For her grounding in theatre, Abigail is indebted to Jacqueline Gunn for whom she has realised many wonderful costume designs. *The Hobbit* was her first major costume design production. As a teacher/facilitator, her experience ranges from children's drama workshops to lecturing on an MA course in scenography. She has worked on annual projects and one-off workshops for a number of higher education institutions, in particular, Croydon College and the Royal Academy of Dance.

Ken Harrison
Ken Harrison studied at the Ruskin School, Oxford and with Motley at Riverside Studios, in London. In 1984 he was awarded an Arts Council bursary to spend a year at Watford Palace Theatre. He has wide-ranging repertory experience and has designed numerous productions for Pitlochry Festival Theatre in the past 12 years. Much of his recent work has involved film and literary adaptations including: *The 39 Steps* (UK tour), *Passport to Pimlico* (UK tour); *Travels with my Aunt* (Nottingham Playhouse), and *The Ladykillers* (UK tour and Pitlochry). Design for new writing includes: *Mindgame* by Anthony Horowitz (Vaudeville Theatre, London); *Parking Lot in Pittsburgh* by Anne Downie (New Byre Theatre, St. Andrews); and the musical *Yee-Haw!!* by Shrubshall and *Free* (Westcliff Theatre and Bromley Theatre).

Becky Hawkins
Graduating from Goldsmiths College in 1990 with a BA Honours (English and Drama), Becky Hawkins then trained in design at Bristol Old Vic Theatre School. During her 11 years as a designer, she has specialised in theatre for young people. She is currently studying part-time for a Masters in art and design. In her home town of Exeter, she has designed *Bouncers, A Passionate Woman* and *Hamlet* in Rougemont Gardens, for the Northcott Theatre, and *Oliver!, The Wizard of Oz* and *The Wind in the Willows* for the Young Company.
Tin Pan Ali, the most recent, was her 40th professional design. For Plymouth Theatre Royal Education, she designed *Brother Jacques, Korczak, The Hot Rock, The Threepenny Opera, Oh! What a Lovely War, Sweeney Todd* and *The Hired Man. Into the Woods, The Rime of the Ancient Mariner, Blood Wedding, The Visit, Shriek-Arena, Macbeth, A Bucket of Eels* and *Custer's Last Stand* were all designs

for Salisbury Playhouse Education. Other designs include: *Frankenstein* (Contact Youth Theatre, Manchester); *Starchild* (Barnstaple); *Can We Afford the Doctor?* (Age Exchange); *The Hobbit* and *The Dispute* (Theatre Royal Bath Education); *The Polychronicon*, a millennium community play (Chester Gateway Theatre) and numerous projects in schools and colleges.

Haworth Tompkins, Architects

Haworth Tompkins was formed in 1991 by architects Graham Haworth and Steve Tompkins. The studio has designed work in the UK and abroad for clients across the public, private and subsidised sectors, including housing, schools, galleries, theatres, offices, shops and factories. Project sizes range from £1m to £150m. Most of the partnership's completed buildings have won major design awards and have been published nationally and internationally. They were named Young Architects of the Year at the 2001 Building Awards and Outstanding Young Architects of 2001 by the Royal Fine Arts Commission, in addition to winning the 2001 English Partnerships Regeneration Award for high density housing. They are developing a reputation for theatre design through completed projects, work in progress, lectures and writing. Their buildings are primarily influenced by the specific chemistry of individual places and cultural situations. What these buildings have in common is an approach rather than a stylistic signature. The architects put enormous effort into understanding the nature of a site and the needs of a building's users, a process which often yields original or unconventional solutions. Sustainability and accessibility are other important criteria for which they have recently won specific design awards. Professionalism underpins the creative work of the studio. The combination of a small, close-knit team, a limited number of projects in development at any one time and wide range of building experience enables them to offer an exceptional level of service to their clients. Their design and studio management systems earned them a place on the shortlist for the 2001 Construction Industry Best Practice award. The evolution of any design involves the use of a number of in-house media including CAD visualisation, model making, 3D prototyping, painting and hand drawing. The majority of their production information is produced using Microstation CAD software and they increasingly exploit the internet as the primary means of communication within the design team and beyond. They remain involved in teaching and research through lecturing, examining and writing.

Simon Holdsworth

Simon Holdsworth trained at Wimbledon School of Art, London and at the Kunstacademie, Maastricht. For theatre, he produced and designed the set and costumes for *Lunch* and *The Bow of Ulysses*, directed by Selena Cartmel at Arch 295, London. Other designs of set and costume include two world premieres for plays by Steven Berkoff: *The Secret Love Life of Ophelia*, directed by the writer and *Ritual in Blood*, directed by Timothy Walker at the Nottingham Playhouse. With the choreographer,

Lea Helmstädter, he devised and designed *Frigidaire*, performed at the Place Theatre, London and then revived for Jump dance festival. He also designed Tchaikovsky's *Eugene Onegin* for Guildford Opera. Working in film, he was the production and costume designer on *Love After a Fashion*, directed by Simon Powell and production designer for the music video *Mr Sunday*, featuring Jackie OnAssid and directed by Paul Hills. He is currently artistic director of the art space, Arch 295 in south London and is a freelance designer.

Pamela Howard

Pamela Howard is a theatre designer, director, writer, educator, exhibition curator and international producer, creating theatre events in many countries and languages. She was awarded a Leverhulme Emeritus fellowship in 1999 to write *What is Scenography?* (Routledge UK/USA in November 2001). She was creator (adapter, director and designer) of *La Celestina*, by Fernando de Rojas, *1492*, at the Hopkins Center, USA in February 2002; the text is to be published by Oberon Books in 2002/3 with future production planned in London and Israel. As a site-specific designer: *The Government Inspector* (Los Angeles USA, May 2002); as creator/director: *ScenOmanifestO* (Rex Cinema, Belgrade, September 2002); as designer: *Victory*, by Howard Barker (Theatre Wspolzecny Wroclaw for the International Festival in 2003); and a new opera for the Northern State Opera Thessaloniki as part of the Greek Cultural Olympics in 2004. In 1999 she produced Opera Transatlantica's *Concerto Barroco* for the London International Festival of Theatre, and in 2001 co-created a new production of *Rondo Adafina* for presentation in London and Caracas in 2002-3 for the same company. She was also curator of two major international exhibitions: *Frantisek Zelenka: Stage Designer, 1904-1944*, shown in - London; and the *Ralph Koltai Retrospective* shown in London, Prague and South East Asia.

Richard Hudson

Richard Hudson was born in Zimbabwe and educated in Zimbabwe and England. He is British Scenography Commissioner to OISTAT and a Royal Designer for industry (RDI). In 1988 he won an Olivier Award for the Jonathan Miller season at the Old Vic (London). His set designs for *The Lion King* have won numerous awards including a Tony in 1998. Recent theatre includes: *'Tis Pity She's a Whore* and *Doctor Faustus* at the Young Vic (London). Recent opera includes: *La Khovantchina* (Paris Opera); *The Cunning Little Vixen* (Opera North); *Of Mice and Men* (Bregenz, Washington, Houston); *Tamerlano* (Florence); *Peter Grimes* (Amsterdam); Mozart/da Ponte trilogy (Glyndebourne). Future projects include *Benvenuto Cellini* (Zurich), *Les Vêpres Siciliennes* (Paris), *Idomeneo* (Florence); Wagner's *Ring Cycle* for ENO.

Rebecca Hurst

Rebecca Hurst trained at the Motley Theatre Design Course in 1999. She is resident designer for Cartoon de Salvo, for which she has designed *Ladies and Gentlemen, Where Am I?*, *Meat and Two Veg* and *Bernie and Clive* (BAC, London and tour).

Other designs include: *Measure for Measure* (Cambridge Arts Theatre); *Taniko* (Queen Elizabeth Hall, London); *Monogamy* (Riverside Studios, London); *Women of Troy* and *This Cookie May Contain Nuts* (Orange Tree Theatre, Richmond); *Logic* (The Chelsea Centre, London); *Solace* (Southwark Playhouse, London); and *Blessings* (The Old Red Lion, London). She has designed four projects for the London Sinfonietta Education Department as well as productions for Mountview Theatre Academy and Oxford School of Drama. She latest design is for *Master Harold and The Boys* for the Bristol New Vic Studio (October 2002).

Jason Durrant Ions

Jason Ions studied at the Motley Theatre Design Course. In 1998 he became resident designer at the Maddermarket Theatre in Norwich. During an 18-month period, his set designs included: *Present Laughter, Translations, The Owl and the Pussycat, Enjoy, Happy Days, Moll Flanders, A Woman of No Importance, Imagine Drowning, Stepping Out, Blithe Spirit, Salonica, Woman in Mind, Wind in The Willows, Fall of the House of Usher, Divers, Load of Old Bowls* and *The Bright and Bold Design*. His freelance credits since then include: *The Glass Menagerie, Dragon Fever* (Eastbound Touring Company); *Spring Awakening* and a series of nine short Beckett plays (University of East Anglia); *Twelfth Night*, (Shakespeare4Kidz, national tour); *One Dark Night, Frog in Love*, (Tiebreak Touring Theatre); *Woyzeck* (Oxford School of Drama). He has just completed his third season as co-designer for the Cromer Pier Seaside Special Shows and teaches stage design and stage management at the University of East Anglia, Norwich.

Neil Irish

Neil Irish trained at City of Birmingham Polytechnic, Slade School of Fine Art and at the National Film School. He was winner of the Leslie Hurry Prize for Stage Design in 1991, and winner of the 1991 Linbury Prize for Stage Design. His credits include: *Accrington Pals* (RADA); *Darkness Falls, Monkey's Paw* (Palace Theatre Watford); *Rita, Sue and Bob Too* (West Yorkshire Playhouse); *An Error of Judgement* (Strathcona Theatre Company); *True Brit* (Birmingham Rep); *Popcorn* (West Yorkshire Playhouse); *Shirley Valentine* (Apollo/Birmingham Stage Co); *The Birds* (Birmingham Promenade Festival); *Timon of Athens* (English Shakespeare Company); *Beauty and Babel The Beast* (Theatre Venture/Stratford East, London); *Noises Off* (Brewhouse Theatre, Taunton); *Hello, Dolly* (Alexandra, Birmingham); *Pinocchio* (Nottingham Playhouse and Teatro Kismet, Bari, Italy); *To Kill A Mockingbird* (Royal Lyceum, Edinburgh, Riverside and tour); *The Love Child, Nicholas Nickleby, The Man Who Was Thursday, Hamlet: First Cut, Poor Mrs Pepys, The Red Princess, Les Miserables, The Aspern Papers, Bartleby The Scrivener* (Red Shift Theatre Company and UK tours); *Waiting For Godot, Hard Times, Twelfth Night, She Stoops To Conquer, Electra, A Doll's House, The Tempest, Wind In The Willows, Dr Jekyll & Mr Hyde* (Compass Theatre Company). Work in opera includes: *Don Giovanni* (Opera

Holland Park); *La Traviata* (Mid Wales Opera); *Letters To Felice, Quest 2: The Good People Try Harder* (The Pavilion Theatre Dublin); *The Beggar's Opera, The Aspern Papers* (Guildhall School of Music and Drama); *Rodelinda, La Vera Costanza or High Fidelity* (Opera Theatre Company); *The Nightingale's To Blame* (Opera North); *Amadigi, I Pagliacci, Frankie's, Wiener Blut as That Dublin Mood* (Opera Theatre Dublin, Buxton Festival, Brooklyn Academy of Music, New York, Portugal, Prague and Melbourne); *A Family Affair, The Man Who Strides The Wind* (Almeida Opera/ENO for Contemporary Opera Studio); National Opera Studio Showcase (Queen Elizabeth Hall); *The Judgement of Paris, Masque of The Devils* (Royal Academy, Queens House, Greenwich). Dance: *The Last Battle* (Peacock Theatre); *4 Mary* (Second Stride). Film: *Daylight Robbery* (Independent Short Film). Television: BBC TV, Birmingham.

Martin Johns

Martin Johns started his career at the Belgrade Theatre, Coventry and became head of design for the Tyneside Theatre Company, York Theatre Royal and the Leicester Haymarket Theatre. During the latter period he designed the set for the West End production of *Me and My Girl* at the Adelphi Theatre and subsequently Broadway, Japan, Australia, South Africa and British and American tours. The design was nominated for a Drama Desk Award and a Tony Award. Other West End shows include: *Masterclass* (Old Vic and Wyndhams); *Passion Play* (Wyndhams); *West Side Story* (Her Majesty's); *The Hired Man* (Astoria); *The Entertainer* (Shaftesbury); *Brigadoon* (Victoria Palace); *A Piece of My Mind* (Apollo); *The Secret Lives of Cartoons* (Aldwych); *Rolls Royce* (Shaftesbury); *Let the Good Stones Roll* (Ambassadors); *Mack and Mabel* (Piccadilly); and the set for *The Romans in Britain* (National Theatre). Recent designs include: *A Different Way Home* and *The True Life Fiction of Mata Hari* (Watford Palace Theatre); *Breaking the Code* (Chester Gateway Theatre); and a re-design of the Kirby Gallery for the Senhouse Museum, Maryport. He designed the 1998 Century Theatre season in Keswick and the models for these shows were shown at the Royal College of Art in the *Time+Space* exhibition of British theatre design. He is now resident designer at the new Theatre by the Lake in Keswick.

Mark Jonathan

Mark Jonathan began lighting in 1973. He worked at Glyndebourne from 1978 until 1992, then became head of lighting at the National Theatre. He has had extensive experience in drama, dance, musicals and opera. Theatre credits include: *The Waiting Room*, directed by Indu Rubasingham; *Skylight*, directed by Richard Eyre; *Titus Andronicus; Adventures of the Stoneheads* (National Theatre); *Clubland* (Royal Court, London); *The Lady's not for Burning*, directed by Sam West (Chichester Festival); *Snake in the Grass* (Old Vic, London); *Jumpers* (Birmingham Rep). Designs for David Bintley at the Birmingham Royal Ballet have included: *Seasons, Giselle, Madding Crowd, Protecting Veil, Prospect Before Us, Powder, Two Pigeons, Dante Sonata, Enigma*

Variations, Scenes de Ballet, Brahms' Waltzes. Future plans include *Beauty and the Beast*. For Stuttgart Ballet he designed *Landschaft und Erinnerung* and *Exilium*. Musicals include: *Honk!* (Olivier Theatre, National Theatre); *Peggy Sue Got Married* (Shaftesbury, London); *Sweet Charity* (Victoria Palace, London); *Marlene* (London, Paris and Broadway); *Ha'penny Bridge* (Eire). Opera credits include: *Peter Grimes, Falstaff, Don Pasquale* (Los Angeles Opera); *Die Entführung aus dem Serail* (Strasbourg); *La Finta Semplice* (Potsdam); *Venus & Adonis, Dido & Aeneas* (Antwerp and Ghent); *Carmen* (Tel Aviv); *Orpheus & Euridice* (Scottish Opera); *The Rake's Progress, Il Barbiere di Seviglia, Entführung, Idomeneo, Cosi fan tutte, Albert Herring* (Glyndebourne Touring Opera); *Seraglio, Gianni Schicchi, Cavalleria Rusticana, Rigoletto, Barber of Seville, Betly, Pagliacci* (Holland Park Opera, London); *Albert Herring* (Rome and Reggio Emilia). His designs were selected for the 1999 Prague Quadrennial.

Richard Jones
Richard Jones was born in London. As director, operatic productions include: *The Queen of Spades* and last year's Olivier Award-winning *Hansel and Gretel* (Welsh National Opera); *The Love for Three Oranges, Die Fledermaus*, David Sawer's new opera *From Morning to Midnight* and *Lulu* (ENO); *Der Ring des Nibelungen* (Royal Opera House - *Evening Standard* Award); *Pelléas and Mélisande* (Opera North and ENO); *Der Fliegende Holländer* and *Jenufa* (Amsterdam); *Julius Caesar*, Opernwelt - Production of the Year, and *The Midsummer Marriage* (Munich); *L'enfant et les Sortilèges* and *Der Zwerg* (Paris); *Un Ballo in Maschera* and *La Bohème* (co-director and designer, Bregenz Festival); *Flight* and *Euryanthe* (Glyndebourne). Theatre credits include: *Too Clever by Half* (Olivier Award), *The Illusion* (Old Vic, London. *Evening Standard* Award); *Into the Woods* (Phoenix Theatre, London. Olivier and *Evening Standard* Awards) Other productions include: *A Flea in Her Ear* (Old Vic); *Le Bourgeois Gentilhomme* (National Theatre); *Black Snow* (American Repertory Theatre); *All's Well That Ends Well* (Public Theatre, New York); *Holy Mothers* (Ambassadors, Royal Court Theatre, London); *La Bête, Titanic* and *Wrong Mountain* (Broadway); *Six Characters Looking For an Author* (Young Vic, London); *A Midsummer Night's Dream* (RSC). In 2000 Richard was awarded the title Designer of the Year with Antony McDonald for *Un Ballo in Maschera* in Germany. In 2001, he was nominated for a *South Bank Show* award for *The Queen of Spades* (WNO) and for an Olivier Award for *Pelléas and Mélisande* (ENO). He was awarded the Barclays/TMA Award 2001 for *The Queen of Spades* (WNO).

Robert Jones
Robert Jones trained at Central School of Art and Design. Design credits include: *Democracy* and *Crossing the Equator* (The Bus Theatre); *A Collier's Friday Night, Bold Girls, You be Ted, Morning & Evening, The Flight Into Egypt Lucky Sods, Back Up The Hearse, Buried Alive* (Hampstead Theatre, London); *Getting Attention* (Royal Court, London); *The Prime of Miss Jean Brodie, When We Are Married, Lautrec, The Killing of Sister George, Jolson* (Canada, USA, Australia); *Rosencratz & Guildenstern are Dead, The Goodbye Girl, The Real Inspector Hound/Black Comedy, Benefactors* (West End); *Uncle Vanya, The Magistrate* (Royal Exchange, Manchester); *Saturday, Sunday, Monday* (Chichester Festival Theatre); *Proposals* (West Yorkshire Playhouse); *York Millennium Mystery Plays* (York Minster); *Divas* (Donmar, London); *Stressed* (Ruby Wax Tour); *The Secret Rapture* (Los Angeles. Drama-Logue Critics' Award); *The Lobby Hero* (Donmar and West End). For the RSC: *Pentecost, The Herbal Bed, Jubilee, Cyrano de Bergerac, Henry VIII* (also Broadway and Washington DC); *Romeo and Juliet, The Merchant of Venice, Jubilee, The Winter's Tale, Othello* and *Eastward Ho!* For the National Theatre: *Look Back In Anger, Playboy of the Western World* and *s* (also West End and Broadway). Opera credits include: *The Elixir of Love* (ENO); *Der Rosenkavalier* (Wuppertal/ Gelsenkirchen); *Manon Lescaut* (Gothenburg Opera). Nominated for Best Costume Design, Olivier Awards 1999 and 2000 for his work on the RSC's *Henry VIII* and *The Winter's Tale*.

Sophie Jump
Sophie Jump trained at Central Saint Martin's College of Art and Design. She works in both theatre and dance and is co-founder of Seven Sisters Group dance company. Work includes: *Full Moon* (Theatr Clwyd, Mold; Young Vic, London and tour); *The Tempest* (Shared Experience tour); *Rape of Lucrece* (Angelus Arts); *Twelfth Night, If I were lifted up from earth, The Tempest, Pericles* (A and BC Theatre Company); *Macbeth, The Caucasian Chalk Circle, Under Milk Wood* (BADA). She has designed the costumes for all Seven Sisters Group pieces, choreographed by Susanne Thomas, which include: *Salome* (St Pancras Chambers, London); *Trainstations* (Kings Cross, Waterloo and other train stations in the UK and abroad); *On Stage* (The Place Theatre, London); *Concrete* (National Theatre); *Removed* (London Contemporary Dance School Library); *Jerwood 10x8 Stairworks, 02* (Wapping Power Station); *Ballroom* (Royal Festival Hall, London); *The Forbidden* (Royal Opera House, Covent Garden). She exhibited in the *Time+Space* (1999) and her work was chosen to form part of the British exhibit at the 1999 Prague Quadrennial. She is also a member of the Equity Designers' Committee.

David Kidd
David Kidd's work covers theatre, corporate and industrial presentations, fashion, concerts and music events. Theatre credits include: *Dick Barton* and *Taming of the Shrew* (Nottingham); *Oleanna* and *Speed-the-Plow* (Birmingham); *Horace, Lighting the Day, Mademoiselle Colombe, The Female Odd Couple* and *Paul Merton* (London and West End). For the National Youth Theatre: *Nicholas Nickleby, The Threepenny Opera* and the HSBC Youth Gala (The Royal Albert Hall). He has collaborated with director Patrick Sandford at Southampton's Nuffield Theatre on numerous productions including: *Twelfth Night, Earth and Sky, The Tempest, John Wayne Principle, Beach Wedding, Oedipus, The Bacchae, The Shagaround, Three Sisters* and *Cyrano de Bergerac*, many of these productions transferring and touring. Tours include: *Bazaar and Rummage, Home Truths* and *Sherlock Holmes*. Concerts include: Monserrat Caballé (Drury Lane); *The Equality Show* (Royal Albert Hall); *Pride* and *The 20th Century Blues Gala*, these events featuring major recording artists. Corporate and fashion presentations include Paul Smith, Antonio Berardi, IBM, Mary Kay Cosmetics and Diesel.

Ralph Koltai
Ralph Koltai studied at the Central School of Art and Design in London and subsequently became head of the Theatre Design Department (1965-72). He has designed some 200 productions of opera, drama, dance and musicals, in the UK and abroad. As associate designer for the RSC he worked on more than 30 productions, including: *Cyrano de Bergerac, Troilus and Cressida* and *Othello*.
Other theatre credits include: an all-male production of *As You Like It* (National Theatre, 1967 and San Francisco/New York, 1975); *Back To Methuselah, State of Revolution, The Guardsman, Brand, Richard III, The Wild Duck, Man and Superman* (National Theatre). Musicals include: *Billy, Bugsy Malone, Dear Anyone, Metropolis, Hair* (West End); *Carrie, My Fair Lady* (Broadway). Work in opera and dance includes: *Tanhäuser, Taverner, The Icebreak* (Royal Opera, Covent Garden); *The Planets* (Royal Ballet); *Mahagonny, Bluebeard's Castle, Carmen*, Wagner's complete *Ring Cycle* (1970-1981), *The Seven Deadly Sins, Anna Karenina, Pacific Overtures* (ENO). Recent work includes: *Genoveva* (Opera North, Leeds); *Don Giovanni* (Mariinsky Theatre, St Petersburg); *Simon Boccanegra* (Welsh National Opera), *Nabucco* (Roman Amphitheatre, Orange); *Dalibor* (Scottish Opera); *A Midsummer Night's Dream* (Gladsaxe Teater, Copenhagen); *Suddenly Last Summer*, for which he was director and designer (Nottingham Playhouse). Plans include: *Katya Kabanova* (La Fenice, Venice). As a director, his work includes: *The Flying Dutchman* and *La Traviata* (Hong Kong Arts Festival, 1987). Ralph Koltai has received national and international awards for his design work including a CBE in 1983. He was part of the Gold Medal-winning team at the 1975 Prague Quadrennial, he won a Silver Medal at PQ'87 and the Golden Troika National Award at PQ'79 and '91. He is a Fellow of The Academy of Performing Arts, Hong Kong, and of Central Saint Martin's College of Art and Design, London. *The Ralph Koltai Retrospective Exhibition* by the London Institute opened in 1997 with the publication *Ralph Koltai - Designer For the Stage* by Lund Humphries.

Anthony Lamble
Theatre includes: *Sing Yer Heart Out For The Lads* (Lyttelton Loft, National Theatre); *The Roman Actor* (The Swan, Stratford on Avon); *Mother Theresa is Dead* and *Herons* (Royal Court, London); *Comedians, The Contractor, Troilus and Cressida* (Oxford Stage Company); *A Christmas Carol* (Chichester Festival Theatre); *A Midsummer Night's Dream, As You Like It* (National Theatre and tour); *In Celebration, The Sea, Aristocrats, Retreat from Moscow, The School of Night, Insignificance, The King of Prussia, Spell of Cold Weather* (Minerva, Chichester); *Barefoot in the Park* (Royal Theatre, Northampton and Watford Palace); *Lettice and Lovage, Exquisite Sister, Burning Everest* (West Yorkshire Playhouse); *Card Boys, All of You Mine, Mortal Ash, Pond Life, Not Fade Away, Evil Doers, Looking at You (Revived Again)* (Bush Theatre, London); *Pippin, Biloxi Blues, The Odd Couple, Dancing at Lughnasa* (National Youth Theatre, Arts Theatre, London); *Heartbreak House, Hamlet, Whole Lotta Shakin', Comedians* (Belgrade, Coventry); *King Baby* (RSC, The Pit, London). He has designed productions for Leicester Haymarket, Sheffield Crucible, Almeida Music Festival, English Touring Theatre, The Gate Theatre, Riverside Studios, Lyric Hammersmith, Croydon Warehouse, Paines Plough, Shared Experience and RNT Studio. Dance and opera credits include: *Facing Viv* for English National Ballet; *Palace in the Sky* (ENO Baylis Programme at Hackney Empire); *L'Orfeo* (Purcell Quartet, tour of Japan 2001). Film includes: *A Secret Audience*. He is a course tutor for the Motley Theatre Design Course.

Stefanos Lazaridis
Stefanos Lazaridis has worked extensively in Britain and abroad, notably in theatre (Chichester Festival Theatre, the West End, Almeida Theatre, RSC) and opera. He has designed more than 30 productions for ENO including: *Rusalka* (also Frankfurt and Rome); *Lady Macbeth of Mtsensk* (also Amsterdam); *Hansel and Gretel* (also Venice and Amsterdam); *Macbeth, Wozzeck, The Adventures of Mr Broucek* (also Munich); *Doctor Faust, Madam Butterfly, The Mikado* (also Los Angeles, Houston, Venice and New York); *Tosca* (also Florence and Houston); and all seven productions in the 2000 Italian Opera Season. He has also designed for the Royal Opera, Scottish Opera and Opera North, the 1988 arena production of *Carmen* at Earl's Court and international tour; and many productions in Europe and the USA. Recent work includes: large-scale productions for the lake stage at the Bregenz Festival of *Der Fliegende Holländer, Nabucco* and *Fidelio* (all produced by David Pountney); *The Greek Passion* (Bregenz Festspielhaus and Royal Opera); *La Fanciulla del West* (La Scala, Milan, Turin and Tokyo); *Pelléas et Mélisande* (Nice); *Werther* (Vancouver); *I Pagliacci* and *Cavalleria Rusticana* (Staatsoper, Berlin); *The Turn of the Screw* (La Monnaie, Brussels); *Moïse et Pharaon* (1997 Rossini Festival at the Palasport, Pesaro); *Katya Kabanova, Faust* (Bayerische Staatsoper, Munich); *Lucia di Lammermoor* (Tel Aviv); *Lohengrin* (Bayreuth Festival); and *Wozzeck* (Royal Opera, Covent Garden). He directed and designed: *Oedipus Rex* (Opera North, Leeds); *Oedipus Rex* and *Bluebeard's Castle, Maria Stuarda* (Scottish Opera); *Orphée et Eurydice* (Australian Opera); *The End of Life* (Athens); and Duran Duran's 1993 *Rock Show* (North American tour). Awards include *London Evening Standard* and Olivier Awards for his work for ENO; Olivier Award for Best Opera Production for *The Greek Passion*; an Olivier nomination for Best Achievement in Opera for the ENO *Italian Opera Season*; the 1998 Opernwelt German Critics' award for Designer of the Year for *Julietta* (Opera North) and *The Turn*

of the Screw (La Monnaie); the 2000 Martinu Foundation Medal for outstanding services to Martinu's operas; and a Diploma of Honour at the 1999 Prague Quadrennial. Future plans include the Athens Olympics in 2004.

Marie-Jeanne Lecca
Marie-Jeanne Lecca was born in Bucharest where she studied at the Beaux Arts Institute. She lives in London and has worked frequently with directors Keith Warner, David Pountney and Francesca Zambello. As a set and costume designer her opera credits include: *Thérèse Raquin* (Dallas, Montreal); *Falstaff, The Stone Guest, Pelleas and Melisande, Moses* (ENO); *Iolanthe* (Scottish Opera); *The Barber of Seville* (Glimmerglass Opera); *The Pirates of Penzance* (D'Oyly Carte); *Carmen* (Minnesota Opera, Seattle Opera, Houston Opera, Teatro Reggio, Turin). She also designed the costumes for: *Turandot* (Salzburger Festspiele); *Macbeth* (Opernhaus Zurich); *Rienzi* and *Jenufa (Wiener Staatsoper); The Greek Passion* (Bregenzer Festspiele and Royal Opera House); *Katya Kabanova* and *Faust* (Bayerische Staatsoper, Munich); *The Turn of the Screw* (La Monnaie, Brussels); *Salammbô* (Opéra National de Paris); *Julietta* (Opera North and Opera Zuid, Maastricht); *The Nose* (De Nederlandse Opera Amsterdam); *Cavalleria Rusticana* and *I Pagliacci* (Staatsoper Unten den Linden, Berlin); *Pacific Overtures, Nabucco*, Verdi's *Requiem* and *Der Freischütz* (ENO); *The Adventures of Mr Broucek* (ENO) and Bayerische Staatsoper, Munich); *La Clemenza di Tito* (Opéra National du Rhin, Strasbourg). Her theatre work includes sets and costumes for: *As You Like It* and *La Bête Humaine* (Nottingham Playhouse); costumes for *The Taming of the Shrew* (RSC); and Napoleon (West End). Current projects are *Guillaume Tell* (Opéra National de Paris); *Wozzeck* (Royal Opera, Covent Garden) and *West Side Story* (Bregenzer Festspiele).

Levitt Bernstein Associates
Levitt Bernstein is an architectural practice with over 25 years experience of working in the arts and cultural sectors, including the design of theatres, galleries and performing arts centres as well as masterplan design for cultural complexes. The practice's approach is to bring fresh thinking to each of its projects and to encourage design innovation based on sound technical expertise. Their work has been recognised with a number of significant architectural awards. Much of the their work in the arts and cultural sector has been funded by the National Lottery and so they are familiar with this process and are able to assist with applications. Above all, Levitt Bernstein brings to each project the desire to consult and debate which, in itself, is a skill developed through a long-standing commitment to ensure that both the commissioner and the end user receive buildings that do far more than simply work well. They must stimulate, excite and address, responsibly, the increasingly important environmental issues as well as being innovative and creatively designed. All of the projects represent a collaboration between designer, client, end user and, frequently, artists.

Alistair Livingstone
At the age of four Alistair Livingstone produced work by 'local kids' on a kitchen table in a garden shed, using a soap packet and the sun's rays, to create a spotlight. Since then he has designed and directed in diverse venues, ranging from a damp basement in Liverpool, to black box spaces in Australia to international opera houses, including The Teatro Colon, Buenos Aires, the Sydney Opera House, and, recently the New National Theatre, Tokyo. He has subverted traditional theatres, by building performance spaces within the auditorium and dug holes in a cricket pitch to create a setting for a military tattoo. He has used the form of a Nautilus Shell to create a demountable membrane structure for the Australian Bicentennial and the intersection of lay lines as the centre point of an ecologically conceived house, Art schools, universities and schools of performance have invited him as a tutor in theatre design, environmental design and fine art. Exhibitions of his designs for the theatre, drawings, paintings, and black and white photographs have been shown in Australia and Europe.
His production company, Livankha Limited, is currently working on a number of film and multi-media projects. He says: 'It has always been the light that has beguiled me.'

Keith Lodwick
Whilst studying at Central School of Speech and Drama, Keith Lodwick became interested in designing in non-theatrical spaces. Much of his work has been site-specific, using the environment to tell the story and involving the audience actively in the production. His stage adaptation and design of Angela Carter's *The Bloody Chamber*, inside Edinburgh's catacombs, won a Herald Angel Award for Outstanding Achievement and was runner up as Best Design for the Total Theatre Awards. His production of Carter's *The Lady of the House of Love* (part of the British Festival of Visual Theatre) was staged in the former bookshop at the BAC. He was born in Shropshire and began his theatrical career as an actor for the Manchester Youth Theatre. He then went to Liverpool Polytechnic to study theatre and film, where he directed and designed *Les Liaisons Dangereuses* and *The House of Bernarda Alba*.
He was based in Bristol for a number of years where he formed his own theatre company, Rear Window Productions, and designed *The Importance of Being Earnest, Don Giovanni, Macbeth and Don Carlos*. Other design work includes: *Is There Life After High School?, Oliver!, Market Day* (A Year of the Artist project in 2000/01), *The Little Prince, Sweeney Todd, Go Back For Murder, If I Were Lifted Up From Earth, Bent* (*Time Out* Critics Choice) and *Take It To The Green Light, Barry!*
He also works for the Theatre Museum, managing the Corporate Hire Department and leading theatre design workshops.

Sophia Lovell Smith
Sophia Lovell Smith has worked in a variety of spaces from schools to main stages, with a particular interest in new writing, devising and site-specific work. She teaches in schools and colleges. She has an honours degree in theatre arts from Bretton Hall, Leeds University. She worked as an actress for 12 years in touring theatre before becoming a designer.
Recent productions include: Handel's *Ariodante*, directed by Stephen Moffit (ENO Baylis Programme); three plays in the Studio Season - *Hello and Goodbye, In Flame* and *Speed-the-Plow*, all directed by Stefan Escreet (Theatre by the Lake, Keswick); *It Was This Big! A Fishy Tale*, directed by Jeremy James (Oxford Playhouse/OTTC); *The Marriage of Figaro* directed by Toby Wilsher (Palace Opera); *Jonah and the Whale*, directed by Louise Warren (The Little Angel Puppet Theatre); *Souls*, directed by Michael Buffong (Theatre Centre); *Girlz 'n' Boyz*, directed by Julia Samuals (Theatre Royal Stratford East); *Blood Wedding*, directed by Philip Osment (Graeae/Contact Theatre, Manchester); *Pinocchio*, directed by Emily Gray (Regent's Park Open Air Theatre/Unicorn, London). Past productions: *Mushroom Man*, directed by Rosamunde Hutt; *The Hungry Grass; River on Fire*, directed by Helena Uren (Kali Theatre/Lyric Theatre, Hammersmith); *The Sisters*, directed by Katarzyna Deszcz (Scarlet Theatre); *The Mamas & the Papas*, directed by Guy Holland (Quicksilver); *Jemima Puddle Duck and her Friends*, directed by Tony Graham (Unicorn); *Millworks*, directed by Sue Buckmaster and Graham Miller (Theatre-rites); *Fossil Woman*, directed by Helena Uren (Alarmist & Shaker Theatre Co); and *Common Heaven*, directed by Rosamunde Hutt (Theatre Centre).

Claire Lyth
Claire Lyth read drama, history and English at Bristol University.
In 2002, she designed *Twelfth Night* for the National Theatre of Norway. In 2001 designs included: *Macbeth* for a tour of India and China, *Picture of Dorian Gray* (Vienna's English Theatre); *The Tempest* (New York State Theater Institute) and *Outer Space, Inner Space* for Exeter University. Other designs: *The Man Who Thinks He's It* (*The Steve Coogan Show*, Lyceum, London); *Goodness Gracious Me* (tour); *Macbeth* and *Twelfth Night* (English Shakespeare Company); *Macbeth* (Residenz Theatre, Munich); *Shoot* (Jermyn Street Theatre, London); *Split Second* (Lyric Theatre Hammersmith); *All's Well That Ends Well* and *Comedy of Errors* (Regent's Park Open Air Theatre, London); *Candida* (The Arts Theatre, London); *Peter Pan* and *The Three Musketeers* (Crucible Theatre, Sheffield); *A Winter's Tale, Macbeth* and *Shirley Valentine* (Everyman Theatre, Liverpool); and *As You Like It* and *Othello* (Ludlow Festival). Opera designs include: *Rigoletto* (Welsh National Opera tour); *Cosi fan tutte* and *The Secret Marriage* (Hong Kong); *Tosca* (Everyman, Liverpool); *One God, One Farinelli* and *The Medium* (BAC, London). Musicals include: *Fungus the Bogeyman* (Belgrade Theatre, Coventry); *My Fair Lady* (Aarhus, Denmark); *Mad and her Dad* (Lyric Theatre, Hammersmith); *Oklahoma!* (national tour); *Rags* (Spitalfields Market Opera, London); *High Spirits* (Bridewell Theatre, London) and *Snow Queen* (Norden Farm Arts Centre, Maidenhead). Claire was head of design at Liverpool Playhouse and Lyceum Theatre, Edinburgh. She has worked in Hong Kong and in Denmark, Germany, USA, Vienna, Beirut.

Ian MacNeil
Theatre credits include: for the Royal Court Theatre, London, *Far Away, Via Dolorosa* (and Broadway); *This is a Chair, Body Talk, Death and the Maiden* (also national tour) and *Plasticine; Afore Night Come* (Young Vic, London); *Albert Speer, Machinal* (National Theatre); *An Inspector Calls* (National Theatre, West End, Broadway and international); *The Ingolstadt Plays, Figaro Gets Divorced, Jerker* (The Gate, London); *Enter Achilles, Bound to Please* (DV8). Opera includes: *Medea* (Opera North); *Tristan and Isolde; Ariodante* (English National Opera and Welsh National Opera); *La Traviata* (Opéra National de Paris); *Il Ritorno d'Ulisse in Patria* (Bavarian State Opera, Munich). Film and television credits include: *Winterreise* (Channel 4); *Eight* (Working Title). In 1999, Ian designed costumes and environments for the Pet Shop Boys album *Nightlife* and staged the world tour following its release. He is an associate producer on the film *The Hours* (Paramount). Awards: Olivier Award for Best Opera (*Tristan and Isolde*); Critics' Circle Award (*Machinal* and *An Inspector Calls*); Olivier Award for Design (*An Inspector Calls*); Tony nomination for Best Design (*An Inspector Calls*, Broadway); *Evening Standard* Award nomination 2001 (*Afore Night Come*).

Roger Maidment
Roger Maidment is currently head of theatre studies at Trinity College Carmathen. *Moll Flanders* was a co-production between Steel Wasp Theatre Company and the BA Theatre Design and Production Course at Trinity. Before moving full-time into higher education, he worked as a freelance designer with a wide range of theatre companies, including: Avon Touring Theatre Company, Chester Gateway, Forest Forge, Solent Peoples' Theatre, NTC, Theatr na n'Og and York Theatre Royal. Roger retains a commitment to touring theatre, particularly to non-theatre venues, and a collaborative approach to theatre making is integral to his work at Trinity.

Alex Marker
Alex Marker graduated from the Wimbledon School of Art (Theatre Design Course) in 2000. His design credits include: *Commanding Voices* (New End, London); *The Bullet, The Lover/Landscape* (Drayton Court); *Three Sisters* (Greenwich Playhouse, London); *The Snow Queen, Helen of Troy* (Questors Theatre, London); *Charlie's Wake* (Finborough, London); *Alchemy of Desire* (Hackney Empire, Studio, London); and *The Tales of Hoffman* (co-designer, Beaufort Opera Company). As design assistant to Nigel Hook he has worked on *One Touch of Venus* (King's Head, London); *Smashed Blue Hills* (New End); and productions for the Theatre Royal York and Buxton Opera Festival.
For television he has worked as a set painter on *The Way We Live Now* (BBC). He co-ordinates the Questors Youth Theatre, a large youth theatre in West London, which has recently turned professional, and has also taught drama and design at various other schools and colleges. He is currently associate designer at the Finborough Theatre.

Nathalie Maury

Nathalie Maury comes from France where she studied art history at the Ecole du Louvre and acting at the Grenier Maurice Sarrazin.
She performed in *La Jalousie du Barbouillé* at the Avignon Festival Off. She spent two years in Belgium where she learned scenography at the Academie Royale des Beaux Arts de Liège, and designed *La Tonnelle* by Hermann Ungar and the musical, *Charlie Brown*. She then went to London to study theatre design at Central Saint Martin's College of Art and Design. Since she graduated, she has assisted Ralph Koltai on the opera *Genoveva* and designed *The Downsizing of Hell* for the Outlaw Theatre Company; *The Marchioness Inquiry* and *Sticks and Stones* for the Gutted Film and Theatre Company and worked as a graduate assistant in scenography at the Laban Centre London. During her studies, she specialised in digital scenography and undertook research on the relationship between performance and computer. She was commissioned by the Hampstead Theatre to create a 3D visualisation of its new building and by the Zaoum Company, a computer animation for *Hamlet*. In September 2002, she went to Montreal for one year to gain more skills in 3D animation and special effects.

Tanya McCallin

Tanya McCallin trained at Central School of Art and Design. After several productions for regional companies and the London fringe, she began a series of productions of new plays for Hampstead Theatre, designing *Sparrowfall, Dusa, Fish, Stas and Vi* (Mayfair Theatre, Paris and MTC, New York); *Abigail's Party* (BBC Film); *Bodies* (Ambassadors Theatre, London and in Amsterdam); *The Elephant Man* (redesigned for the National Theatre); *The Hard Shoulder* (Aldwych, London); *Sufficient Carbohydrate* (Albery, London); *The Perfectionist* and *A Little Like Drowning*. Other productions include: *Macbeth, Uncle Vanya, Betrayal* and *Mourning Becomes Electra* (Melbourne Theatre Company); *Dread, They Are Dying Out, Don Juan Returns From The Wars* and *Who's Afraid of Virginia Woolf?* (National Theatre); *A Nightingale Sang, Before The Party* (also Apollo) and *Women Beware Women* (Oxford Playhouse); *Ghosts* (Actors Company); *The School For Scandal, Waiting For Godot, The Changeling, The Homecoming, I Am Who I Am* and *The Late Christopher Bean* (Cambridge Theatre Company); *Travelling North* (Lyric Theatre Hammersmith); *My Mother Said I Never Should* (Royal Court, London); *Uncle Vanya* (Vaudeville, London); *Exchange* (Nuffield Theatre, Southampton and Vaudeville, London); *The Winter Wife* (Nuffield and Lyric Theatre. Nomination for TMA Best Design Awards 1991); *Ride Down Mount Morgan* (Wyndham's, London); *Obsession* and *Strictly Entre Nous* (BAC, London); *Hamlet* and *Richard III* (Regent's Park Open Air Theatre, London); *Tolstoy* (Plymouth Theatre Royal and Aldwych, London); *Ancient Lights* (Hampstead Theatre); and *The Recruiting Officer* (Chichester).
She has designed the costumes for *After the Fall* (National Theatre); *Make and Break* (Kennedy Center, USA); *The Perfect Ganesh* (West Yorkshire Playhouse); *Steaming* (Piccadilly,

London); and *Fool for Love* (Donmar Warehouse, London). Her opera work includes: *The Barber of Seville* (ENO and Barcelona); *Manon* (ENO and Dallas Opera); *Macbeth* (Mariinsky, St Petersburg, Covent Garden, Kennedy Center and Baden Baden); and the costumes designs for *Der Rosenkavalier* (Scottish Opera and Opera North); and *Rigoletto* (Royal Opera House, Covent Garden, video and DVD). Tanya has been closely associated with the theatre design department at Central Saint Martin's and was external examiner 1996 - 2000.

Antony Mcdonald

Antony Mcdonald trained as a designer in London on the Motley design course. He and Richard Jones co-directed and designed *La Bohème* for the 2002 and 2001 Bregenz Festivals; *Un Ballo in Maschera* for the 1999 and 2000 Bregenz Festivals and *Der Zwerg* and *L'Enfant et Les Sortilegès* for Paris Opera in 1999. In autumn 2002 he designed Richard Jones' *Giulietta* for the Paris Opera. Solo design and direction credits include: *Aida, Samson et Dalila, Broken Strings* and *Snatched by the Gods* and *The Makropulos Case* all for Scottish Opera. He also created *The Country Wife, Nine Plays by Gertrude Stein* and *The Birthday Party* for the Glasgow Citizens' Theatre. In 2003 he will direct a new production of *King Priam* for the Netherlands' Nationale Reisopera and *Wonderful Town*, the musical, for Grange Park Opera. Other productions include: *A Midsummer Night's Dream, A Merry Widow* (Metropolitan Opera, New York); *Ariadne auf Naxos* (Munich); *Billy Budd* (ENO); *The Trojans* (Opera North, Scottish Opera and Welsh National Opera) all with director Tim Albery. His many designs for dance include recently: *Manoeuvre*, choreographed by Patrick Lewis (English National Ballet); costumes for *Of Oil and Water* for Siobhan Davies; *Hidden Variables* for Ashley Page (Royal Opera House, Covent garden); and the widely acclaimed *Fearful Symmetries*, which won the 1995 Olivier Award for dance.

Peter McKintosh

Theatre includes: *The Merry Wives of Windsor, Pericles, Alice in Wonderland and Through The Looking Glass* (all for the RSC); *Romeo and Juliet* (Washington DC); *Honk!* (Olivier Theatre, National Theatre, UK tour, Boston, Chicago, Tokyo and Singapore); *Widowers' Houses* (Cottesloe Theatre, National Theatre); *Divas at the Donmar* (Donmar Warehouse, London); *Boston Marriage* (Donmar and New Ambassadors, London); *Guys and Dolls* (Crucible Theatre Sheffield); *The Comedy of Errors, Half a Sixpence* (West Yorkshire Playhouse); *Strangers on a Train* (UK tour); *Pal Joey* (Chichester Festival Theatre); *Five Kinds of Silence* (Lyric Theatre Hammersmith); *Demons and Dybbuks* (Young Vic, London); *Buried Alive, The Black Dahlia, Demons and Dybbuks, The Cherry Orchard* (Method & Madness UK tour) Opera includes: the world première of *The Handmaid's Tale* (Royal Danish Opera, Copenhagen); *The Marriage of Figaro, L'Elisir d'Amore* (Mid Wales Opera); *The Barber of Seville, Betly/I Pagliacci* (Holland Park Opera). Dance includes: *Cut To The Chase* (English National Ballet). Forthcoming projects: *The Handmaid's Tale* (ENO).

Fred Meller

Fred Meller was educated at the University of Ulster and the Welsh College of Music and Drama and won an Arts Council design bursary. Recent work includes: *Life with an Idiot* (National Theatre Studio at the Gate Theatre. Jerwood Young Designers' Award); site-specific productions for the Almeida: *Caledonian Road, Ghost Ward, The Whizz Kid* and *Into Our Dreams* (Year of the Artist); *Mincemeat Cardboard* (Citizens' Theatre at the Jam Factory); *Great Expectations* (Unicorn Theatre, London); *The Ghost Downstairs* (Nuffield Theatre); *A Warning to The Curious, David Copperfield, The Wuffings, Site Specific* (Eastern Angles); *The Body of a Woman is a Battlefield in the Bosnian War* (Young Vic, London); *Philistines* (Bloomsbury Theatre, London); *Winner Takes All* (Orange Tree, Richmond); *Death and the Maiden* (Watermill Theatre, Newbury); *Variety*, by Douglas Maxwell, commissioned by the Edinburgh International Festival (Grid Iron Theatre). Fred exhibited at the 1999 Prague Quadrennial. She was recently awarded a fellowship by the Arts Foundation (Scenography) and is taking part in a British Council Theatre Exchange with China. She is a senior lecturer at CentralSaint Martin's College of Art and Design.

Lucinda Meredith

Lucinda Meredith has worked as a stage designer in since 1995 and since 1999 her work has been based in Scotland. For The Arches Theatre Company: *A Midsummer Night's Dream* (The Citizens' Theatre, Glasgow and touring the Highlands and islands); *Juno and the Paycock* (The Citizens' Theatre); *The End Part One*, by Ewan McColl and *The End Part Two*, by Heiner Müller, *Playboy of The Western World, Four Dogs and a Bone*, by Patrick Shanley and *Lord Byron's Love Letter* (The Arches Theatre); *Celle La*, devised (Tramway, Glasgow), and *Prologue*, also devised (Belfast Festival). For Theatre Cryptic: *The Play of The Wather* by Edwin Scriven, and *Nutshell* (The Underbelly, Edinburgh Festival); *David Leddy's On the Edge* (The Pleasance, Edinburgh Festival); *A Little Sexy Something in Between*, devised; *Economical Truth* (The Oval, London) and *The Fire Parade* (Lisbon Expo) with NVA Organisation. Lucinda also works as a project manager with design-driven projects including: Intervention, Scotland's only Fashion Festival; Glasgow's Theatre Design Summer School; The Circus School; and The Festival of New Scottish Theatre. She manages a commission scheme to encourage cross-media theatre practice, in Glasgow: The New Work Season.

Madeleine Millar

Madeleine studied theatre design at Trent Polytechnic, Nottingham and has an MA in Art and Design from Leeds Metropolitan University. She has spent over 20 years in children's theatre, theatre in education, community and repertory theatre. Productions include: *Gaslight, Macbeth, Hedda Gabler, Confusions*, and *Mother Goose* (as a season at St Andrews); *Simple Simon* (Stephen Joseph Theatre-in-the-Round, Scarborough); *Don't She Look Silly* (York Young People's Theatre); *Pentabus, Mutiny on the Bounty, Face at the Window, No Smoke without Walter* (Soapbox Children's Theatre);

Flags and Bandages, Strathnever, Seizing the Time (Leeds Playhouse TIE); *Graven Images, Mountains on the Moon, Bloodlines, Sweet Banana Fruit Mix* (Pit Prop); *Sacred Ground* (Watford Palace TIE); *The Best* (Red Ladder); *Aladdin, The Night Garden, Glory, The Union, The Picture Writer* (Theatr Powys); *The Good Soldier, The Marvellous Boy* (Public Parts); *The Wrench* (Big Brum TIE); *Monsters of Creation* (Collar and TIE); *Fairground Attractions, Sea Changes* (Interplay); *The Boatbuilder - a Tapestry of Tales* (Whitewood and Fleming Theatre and Music); *Edible City, Tidelines* (West Yorkshire Playhouse Theatre in Schools); *One Big Blow* (Compact); *Lighting the Day* (Birmingham Stage); *The Sorcerer's Apprentice, Doctor Faustus* (TAG); *The Bicycle Bridge* (Rejects Revenge). For television: *Series X, Y* and two Christmas episodes of *Last of the Summer Wine* (BBC Entertainment).

Martin Morley

Martin Morley trained at Wimbledon School of Art: 1963-1966. On gaining his Dip.A.D. he was awarded an Arts Council bursary to work as a design assistant at the Royal Lyceum Theatre, Edinburgh. While there, he designed *Juno and the Paycock, The Ha-Ha* and *Death of a Salesman*, all for Richard Eyre. From 1969-72 he was head of design at the Liverpool Playhouse, designing a wide range of plays from Shakespeare to Bond, with directors who included Antony Tuckey, Barry Kyle and Andrew Dallmeyer.
There then followed a lengthy period as designer for Cwmni Theatr Cymru (1973-84). There he learnt the skills of designing touring productions for a wide range of ill-matched venues. The repertoire was mainly in Welsh and ranged from contemporary writing to translations of European classics.
In 1984 he went freelance and also branched out into television design, which now dominates his output - notably *Hedd Wyn* (BAFTA Cymru 1993 with Jane Roberts for Best Design) and a string of drama series and assorted other programmes for S4C. During this period he has designed several productions for Theatr Gwynedd, Bangor, including *Pwy Sy'n Sal* (a Molière double bill) directed by Graham Laker and Firenza Guidi (exhibited in *Time+Space*) and *Dyn Hysbys* (*Faith Healer* by Brian Friel) directed by Sian Summers (exhibited in *Time+Space* and at the 1999 Prague Quadrennial).
www.users.globalnet.co.uk/-rmorley

Ruari Murchison

Ruari Murchison has designed productions at the Stratford Festival (Canada), Stuttgart (Germany), Lucerne (Switzerland), Haarlem (Holland). London work includes productions at the National Theatre, The Royal Opera, Royal Court, Greenwich, Hampstead and The Young Vic (all London). He has also worked at Nottingham Playhouse, West Yorkshire Playhouse, Theatr Clwyd, Birmingham Rep and Bristol Old Vic. Designs include: *The Waiting Room, The Red Balloon, Frozen* (National Theatre); *A Busy Day* (Lyric, Shaftesbury Avenue, London); *Peggy Sue Got Married* (Shaftesbury Theatre, London); *The Snowman* (Peacock, London); *West Side Story* and *The Sound of Music* (Stratford Festival); *Hamlet* (Birmingham Rep, national tour and Elsinore, Denmark); *Peter Grimes,*

Cosi fan tutte (Lucerne Opera); *La Cenerentola, Il Barbiere di Siviglia* (Garsington); *The Protecting Veil* (Birmingham Royal Ballet); *Landschaft und Erinnerung* (Stuttgart Ballet).

Kimie Nakano
Kimie Nakano studied theatre costume at ENSATT in Paris and theatre design at Wimbledon School of Art in London. She trained in costume and theatre design at Opéra de Paris and co-ordinated productions between Opéra de Paris and Saito Kinen Festival in Japan 1997-1999, including those by Robert Wilson, Francesca Zambello and Robert Lepage. She designed the award-winning *Yabu no naka* directed by Mansai Nomura at the Japan Art Festival 1999 and collaborated with Megumi Nakamura on *Sandflower*, which received the Gold Award in the Maastricht Festival 2000 in The Netherlands. Theatre credits include: *Kensuke Kingdom, Big Magic* (Polka Theatre, London); *Sumidagawa* (The Britten Festival); *Rashomon* (Riverside Studios, London); *Double Tongue* (Old Red Lion, London); *Lady Aoi* (New End Theatre, London); *A Midsummer Night's Dream* (Tom Allen Centre, London); *Futon and Daruma* (Wimbledon Theatre Studio); *The Picture of Dorian Gray* (BAC, London); and *Groove* (Unity Theatre, UK tour); *Toute L'eau...*(Théâtre de l,Echangeur, Paris). Director credits include: *The Workshop of Snow* (ENO Studio); *Sandflower* (Den Haag); *Rooms* (Wimbledon School of Art); and *Musubu* (video installation at Surrey Arts Centre).

Dody Nash
Dody Nash initially trained in fine art, studying with the painter Cecil Collins, before completing a degree in history of art (York) and postgraduate theatre design studies (Motley, 1995).
She began her design career assisting leading designers and artists on secondment from the production department of ENO, whilst also working independently on projects in a wide range of media, including theatre, advertising, film and musicals.
More recently she has specialised in music and movement based projects and has completed design commissions for Rambert Dance Company's 75th Anniversary Season: *Twin Suite 2* (Linbury Studio, Royal Opera, Covent Garden and Sadler's Wells); devised work for Sheffield Children's Festival (Opera North); *The Martyrdom of Saint Magnus* (The Opera Group, UK tour). In 2001 she was invited to join the second Royal Designers for Industry (RDI) Summer School, at Dartington Hall in Devon. Dody continues her relationship with ENO with designs for *The Early Earth Operas*, a cycle of children's operas currently in development.

Jennie Norman
Jennie Norman trained at Bath Academy of Art and Bristol Old Vic Theatre School. Designs for European dance and aerial ballet include: *Der Schrei des Kardinals, Wien Wien du bist Allein, Winterreise* (Tanz Theater Wien Vienna); *Caravaggio* (Volksoper, Vienna); *Die Gegeneinladung*, choreographer Liz King (Heidelberger Ballet); *Fool Time, Traume vom Fliegen*, choreographer Helen Croker (Aerial Ballet Münchener Biennale with Cirque Media); *Death of a Faun*, by David Pownall, a new play about Nijinsky. She formed Antidote Theatre with writer, Steve Volk, and director, Caroline Maynard, using new writing as the basis for strong visual theatre. Productions include: *Answering Sprits*, by Steve Volk; *Waiting for Stoppard*, by Miles Kington. She teaches and designs for the University of Bristol Department of Drama where work has included: *Six Characters in Search of an Author* (director George Brandt); *Ivanov* (director Oliver Neville); *The Battle, Jet de Sang, Murderer Hope of Women* (director Gunter Berghaus); *Lark Rise, Teendreams, The Witch, Eastwood Ho!, The Roman Actor, Believe as you List, Love's Sacrifice* (director Martin White); a reconstruction of a Jacobean indoor theatre from drawings by Inigo Jones with director, Martin White. She has taught design aspects on mediaeval theatre, *The Mary Play: From Creation to Nativity* from the Townsley or Wakefield Cycles (director John Marshall); radical theatre: *The Iron Ship*; site-specific work on the SS Great Britain (director Baz Kershaw); 20th-century theatre: *The Possibilities, Spooks*; devised theatre including: *Who Was Changed and Who Was Dead, Wave* (director Simon Jones); *Thirteen Clocks* (with director Jaraslava Siktancova from DAMU Prague). Other teaching has included Bristol Old Vic Theatre School, Bath University Architecture Department and Southampton College of Art. Related work includes: *Wildscreen*; historical television plays on Jenner and Cabot; and collaborations with architects.

Francis O'Connor
Francis O'Connor trained at Wimbledon School of Art. Recent work includes: *The Tempest*, with Richard Briers, *The Plough and the Stars* (Abbey Theatre, Dublin); *The Daughter-in-Law* (Young Vic, London); *The Good Father* and *Sive* (Druid Theatre, Galway); *The Lieutenant of Inishmore* (RSC and Garrick Theatre, London); *Romeo and Juliet* and *As You Like It* (Regent's Park Open Air Theatre); *Communion* (Peacock, Dublin); and *Maometto II* (Opéra National du Rhin, Strasbourg).
Other work includes: the National Theatre of Brent's *The Wonder of Sex* (National Theatre); *My Brilliant Divorce* (Druid Theatre); *Andorra* (Young Vic); *Sondheim's Putting It Together* (Chichester Festival Theatre); *Too Late For Logic* (Lyceum, Edinburgh); *Fortunio* (Grange Park Opera); and *A Raisin In The Sun* (Salisbury Playhouse and Young Vic). Productions for Druid Theatre Company in Galway include: the award-winning *The Beauty Queen of Leenane* (Royal Court, London; Walter Kerr Theatre, New York - four Tony Awards on Broadway; Toronto, Sydney and Dublin) and *Lonesome West* (also London, Dublin, and Lyceum, New York). Many productions for the Abbey, Dublin including: *Iphigenia* and *Big Maggie* (Best Designer Award, *Irish Times* Theatre Awards, 2002); *The Colleen Bawn* and *Tarry Flynn* (both also National Theatre); Tom Murphy's *The House; The Wake* (also Edinburgh Festival); and Brian Friel's *Freedom of the City* (also Lincoln Center, New York).
Other theatre includes: *Peer Gynt* (National Theatre); *La Cava, Two Pianos Four Hands, Anna Weiss* (London's West End); *Love Upon The Throne* (National Theatre of Brent); *Closer* (National Theatre on tour); and *Sacred Heart* (Royal Court).

Christopher Oram
Christopher Oram trained at Wimbledon School of Art. For the Crucible Theatre he has designed *Richard III, Don Juan, Edward II, The Country Wife, Six Degrees of Separation, As You Like It* (also Lyric Hammersmith), *Twelfth Night* and *What the Butler Saw*. At the Donmar Warehouse work includes: *Privates on Parade, Merrily We Roll Along, Passion Play* (also at the Comedy Theatre) and *Good*. These productions were all collaborations with Michael Grandage. Other work includes Grae Cleugh's first play, *Fucking Games*, at the Royal Court (London) and the world première productions of Edward Albee's new plays, *The Marriage Play* and *Finding the Sun* (National Theatre). Also at the National Theatre, Trevor Nunn's production of Gorky's *Summerfolk*. For the Almeida, Christopher designed Michael Grandage's productions of Marlowe's *The Jew of Malta* and Shaw's *The Doctor's Dilemma* (both of which went on national tours). Other credits include *Dinner With Friends* (Hampstead Theatre); A Streetcar Named Desire (Bristol Old Vic); *A Life* (Abbey Theatre, Dublin) and *Aristocrats* (Gate Theatre, Dublin and New York). Earlier this year, Christopher worked on John Caird's production of *Twelfth Night* for the Royal Dramatic Theatre, Sweden.

Keith Orton
Keith Orton trained at Central School of Speech and Drama and graduated in 1992, then freelanced as a stage designer for a number of years, mainly in the Manchester area. This included two years as resident designer at Oldham Coliseum Theatre. During this period he designed national tours of *Little Shop of Horrors* and *Josephine* and designed main house, studio and community productions that included the premiere of *Sylvia's Wedding* by Jimmy Chinn. He returned to Central to become a design tutor in 1997, working on undergraduate courses with both with the production, art and design, and drama in education departments. This has given him the opportunity to evaluate his own process whilst tutoring students in theirs. The role there has combined both teaching stage design and designing for many of the school's public productions. Examples include studio productions of *Angels in America, Six Degrees of Separation, A Clockwork Orange* and *Marat/Sade*; in the Embassy Theatre, productions of *Macbeth, Present Laughter* and *Secret Rapture*; and site-specific productions of *Jabberwocky, Myth Breakers* and *Beowulf* at the Minack Theatre in Cornwall. His latest collaboration was *Sweeney Todd*, which re-launched the newly refurbished Embassy Theatre.

Roma Patel
Roma Patel graduated from at Wimbledon School of Art in 1998 and then gained a Masters degree in scenography at the Birmingham Institute of Art and Design.
She received the Emma Jessop Phillips Award for her final MA project, an interactive multimedia CD-ROM that illustrated the process and the implications of applying computer techniques in the design of sets, costumes and props. Her work has been exhibited at several venues and she has presented papers on the subject in Britain and Germany.
She now works as a freelance scenographer and continues to develop practical techniques to integrate computer technology with the set designer's practice. She has recently been experimenting with remote co-operative working techniques through the use of virtual reality modelling and the internet.
Her most recent work includes designs for the Post Office Theatre Company, *The Farsido* (Tricycle Theatre, London) and for LIFT 2001, *Skeletons of Fish* (Riverside Studios, London). She also teaches workshops in digital set and costume design at Central Saint Martin's College of Art and Design, London and was the resident artist at Wellington College, Berkshire in 2001.

Michael Pavelka
Michael Pavelka trained at Wimbledon School of Art, where he has since returned to lead the theatre design course. He has designed some 150 productions, most of which have been new plays or new musicals. His work includes two shows for the late Lindsey Anderson: *The Fishing Trip* and Holiday (Old Vic Theatre, London). Also *The Life of Galileo* (Best Design *Manchester Evening News* Theatre Awards), *A Midsummer Night's Dream* (Best Production *Manchester Evening News* Awards) also *The Resistible Rise of Arturo Ui* and *The Caucasian Chalk Circle* (Library Theatre, Manchester). His ongoing work with Edward Hall and Propeller Company includes productions of *Twelfth Night, Henry V* and the adaptation of Henry VI plays, *Rose Rage*, at the Watermill Theatre (Newbury), Theatre Royal Haymarket (London) and overseas tour.
Other work in the West End includes: *Macbeth, The Constant Wife, How the Other Half Loves, Other People's Money* and *Leonardo; Blues in the Night* was performed in Dublin, New York, Tokyo after two West End seasons. In 1998 Michael co-produced a Young People's Shakespeare Festival in Ulaanbaatar, Mongolia and has since designed *Mother Courage and Her Children*, in Kampala, at the Kennedy Center, Washington DC and Grahamstown Festival, South Africa. Designs for the RSC include: *The Odyssey, Two Gentlemen of Verona, Henry V* and *Julius Caesar*.

Celia Perkins
Celia Perkins trained in theatre design at Croydon College and at the Slade School of Fine Art in costume design, and construction and set design.
On leaving college, she worked on fringe productions and small-scale touring shows, subsequently working as a scenic artist at the Library and Forum Theatres in Manchester and at the Oldham Coliseum Theatre. Celia has been Resident Designer at the Oldham Coliseum Theatre for the past six years, designing for a wide variety of productions from the ubiquitous annual treat that is pantomime, to the straight and comedy plays, musicals and two-handers, constantly reinventing ways of using a proscenium space with notoriously difficult sightlines.

Dana Pinto
Dana Pinto studied theatre design at Wimbledon School of Art and received the Emma Jesse Phipps Scholarship for her studies on the MA in scenography at Birmingham Institute of Art and Design. Set designs include: *Harmony in Harlem* (musical at George

Wood Theatre, Goldsmith's College, London) and *This Happy Breed* (Man in The Moon, London). Costume designs include: *Two In One, Romeo and Juliet* (Edinburgh Festival 2002 and Polimedia Theatre, Korea with companies Shin Production, SMG Pai Production & Institute, and Komedia UK); *Write This Rhythm: Love* (dance at Bloomsbury Theatre, London); *Fruitilious Crew; Pajazz; Para Chick, Para Flicks; Freestyle* and *Infiltrate the Second Tape* (dance at Paddington Arts, London). Set and costume designs include: *Protest* (Old Vic, London); *NITRObeat* (Queen Elizabeth Hall and Purcell Room, London; Contact Theatre Manchester); *One Dance Will Do* (Theatre Royal Stratford East, London and touring); Ned Rorem operas *Fables, Bertha* and *Three Sisters Who Are not Sisters* (Bridewell, London); and *Hess - The Prince of Spandau* (Barraca Teatro Lisbon). Dana is a trustee of TimeZone Theatre Company looking at the gender roles within performance as well as within the production crew. She received the Asian Kapis (Shell) Award in 2000 for Best Young Achiever in the Arts.

Bruno Poet
Bruno Poet's recent credits include: *Tree Finger Soup*, Rambert Dance Company; *Antarctica* (Savoy Theatre, London); *Les Blancs* and *The Homecoming* (Royal Exchange, Manchester); *The Birthday Party, Sexual Perversity in Chicago* and *The Shawl* (Crucible Theatre, Sheffield); *Island of Slaves, Pleasure Palaces* and *Hansel and Gretel* (Lyric Theatre Hammersmith); *So Long Life* and *The External* (Theatre Royal Bath and tour); *Love's Labours Lost* and *The Cherry Orchard, Don Juan* and *The Taming of the Shrew* (English Touring Theatre); *Cherished Disappointments in Love* (Sphinx/Soho Theatre, London); *Neville's Island* (Watford Palace), *The Lodger* (Windsor and Bromley); *Royal Supreme* and *Musik* (Plymouth Theatre Royal); *Al Murray. The Pub Landlord* (Playhouse Theatre, London) and *Tess of the D'Urbevilles* (Savoy) Recent opera and dance credits include: *Die Zauberflöte, La Gazzetta* and *Intermezzo* (Garsington Opera); *Orfeo ed Euridice* (Opéra National du Rhin); *Macbeth* (North Jutland Opera Company); *Moment to Moment* (Walker Dance Company); *The Turn of the Screw* (Brighton Festival); *Vanessa* (Bloomsbury, London); *Norma* (Barcelona); *La Traviata* and *Fidelio* (English Touring Opera); *Ottone* (Britten Theatre, Royal College of Music); *Hansel and Gretel* (Wilton's Music Hall, London) and a dance piece, *Tweed Venus* (Traverse Theatre, Edinburgh and tour). Future productions include: *King Lear* (ETT); *Just Between Ourselves* (tour); *The Marriage of Figaro* and *Orpheus In The Underworld* (British Youth Opera, Queen Elizabeth Hall); *Babette's Feast* (Linbury Studio, Royal Opera House); *Berlin to Broadway* (Denmark); *Fidelio* (De Vlaamse Opera). In his fifth season with Garsington Opera, he is lighting *La Gazza Ladra, Don Giovanni* and the Janacek double bill *Sarka* and *Osud*.

Christopher Richardson
Christopher Richardson trained at the Royal College of Art under Sir Hugh Casson. He won the silver medal for experimental theatre design and during that time was part of the team that won the *Prix d'Étranger* at the Paris Biennale of 1965. He taught design

and drama in Rutland for 20 years and ran the Uppingham Theatre there for 12 years. He has designed many plays both in the UK and abroad supporting performers such as Rowan Atkinson, Stephen Fry, Mollie Sugden and Max Wall, and the National Youth Music Theatre. He was chairman of the Society of British Theatre Designers for eight years. He now runs Theatre Futures, a theatre consultancy, whose work has included the Theatre by the Lake, Keswick, the Jersey Opera House and the last refurbishment of the Young Vic, London. He is the founder and Director of the Pleasance Theatre Festival in both London and Edinburgh.

John Risebero
John Risebero trained in theatre design at Central Saint Martin's College of Art and Design, graduating in 2000. His recent designs include: *Closer* (ADC Theatre, Cambridge); *The Barber of Seville* (Linbury Studio, Royal Opera, Covent Garden); *Golden Boy* (Yvonne Arnaud Theatre, Guilford and UK tour); *Heroes* (Blue Elephant Theatre); *Hamlet* and *Macbeth* (touring the Lot Valley, France). While studying, he was selected to design the Philip Lawrence Awards 1999 ceremony for the Home Office (Cochrane Theatre) with dancers from the Central School of Ballet. Alongside his own work, he has worked on numerous productions as design assistant. These include: *Follies* (Royal Festival Hall); *Whistle Down the Wind* (UK tour); *Ghosts* (Comedy Theatre, London), *A Little Night Music* and *On Your Toes* (Leicester Haymarket). www.johnrisebero.co.uk.

Cathy Ryan
Cathy Ryan studied fine art at Bristol Polytechnic and post-graduate theatre design at the Bristol Old Vic Theatre School. Credits include: *Strange Fruit, City Echoes, Take My Husband* and *It's a Bobby's Job* (Liverpool Playhouse); *The Conduct of Life, Struggle of the Black Man and the Dogs, Vera Baxter, The Struggle* (Gate Theatre, London); *Streetwalkers* (Bush Theatre, London); *Weissman and Copperface* (Traverse Theatre, Edinburgh); *Loot* (Swan Theatre, Worcester); *Heimerbell* (BAC Young Directors Award); *Fen* and *Masterpieces* (Theatre Royal Stratford East); *Pretend We're Friends* (Quicksilver Theatre for Children); *Of Mice and Men, In Bed with Billy Cotton, Relatively Speaking, Romeo and Juliet, Good Golly Miss Molly, The Good Companions, It's a Lovely Day Tomorrow, Twelfth Night, Millennium Mysteries* (nominated for Barclay's/ TMA award for Best Design); *Mother Goose* (Belgrade Theatre, Coventry); *Turn of the Screw* (Belgrade and Windsor Theatre Royal); *Too Much Too Young* (London Bubble and tour); *Romeo and Juliet, The Good Companions, Dangerous Corner, David Copperfield, When the Wind Blows* and *Thark* (New Vic Theatre, Stoke); *The Cunning Little Vixen* (ENO Baylis Programme); *The Marriage of Figaro* (Pimlico Opera); *Way Past Cool* (Royal Court Young People's Theatre); *Flat 4D, The Gap, Stop the Rot* and *What a Life* (Cardboard Citizens and Deaf Theatre Forum at London Bubble). Film and television work includes: *Riff Raff, Ladybird Ladybird, Young Soul Rebels, Institute Benjamenta* and *Brookside*.

Emma Ryott
Emma Ryott trained at Trent Polytechnic. Credits as assistant costume designer and supervisor include: *The Merry Widow* (Metropolitan Opera, New York); *Il Ritorno d'Ulisse in Patria* (San Carlo Opera, Lisbon); *Cheating, Lying, Stealing* and *Hidden Variables* (Royal Ballet); *A Doll's House* (L'Odéon, Paris); *Porgy and Bess, Francesca da Rimini, Ein Maskenball* (Bregenz Festival); and over 100 productions for the RSC. Her own design credits include: *Twelfth Night* (RSC); *The Entertainer* (Hampstead Theatre, London); *Macbeth* (USA tour); Roald Dahl's *Revolting Rhymes Concert* (BBC Wales); *Manon Lescaut* (associate costume designer, ENO); *Nine* (Malmö Musikteater); *Manon Lescaut* (Gothenburg Opera); *La Bohème* (co-costume design, Bregenz Festival).

Scale Project
Simon Daw and Paul Burgess set up Scale Project in 2000. It uses a multimedia fusion of visual art and theatre to investigate a specific theme. The current subject, explored through factual research and artistic responses, is new towns, real and ideal, and the lives of their inhabitants. Structured as a series of collaborations with artists, performers and members of the public, it originally focused on two specific urban communities: the 'new town' of Harlow (UK), where it staged a performance in the town hall and civic square, and Novosibirsk (Siberia). Projects in Novosibirsk included work with the Wampeter dance group in a nuclear bunker. Collaborations are based on the idea of performers and designers working together directly and a shared belief that design, performance and text carry equal weight. Paul and Simon trained at Motley Theatre Design Course. Simon had studied fine art at Glasgow School of Art, while Paul read English at Oxford. Both also work independently as theatre designers, and between them have worked in venues ranging from London to Tokyo and New York.

Vivienne Schadinsky
Vivienne Schadinsky studied at Motley Theatre Design Course. Current themes in her work include the uses of media with projection in performance. Her research and development explore the use of modern technologies in traditional theatre, site-specific work, dance and devised plays. Theatre and costume designs include: *London/My Lover* (ICA, London); *Primaries* (Young Vic Studio, London); and *Malcontent* and *Revenger's Tragedy* (Pentameters, London). Costume design: *The Dreamcatcher* (Unicorn Theatre) and micro compact car Smart advertising promotion. Audio-visual and screen design: *Blavatsky* (Young Vic Studio) and *Here's what I did with my body one day* (Alwych tube station). Film work as art director includes: commercials for Smirnoff Ice, Napster, Harper Collins; the short film, *Ghost Child* (Channel 4); and as assistant art director, *Randall and Hopkirk (Deceased)* for BBC; *La Luna* (Channel 4). Other work includes: decoration for Birds Eye Fishfingers for launch of commercial; foyer design for Tara Arts: *Journey to the West* (national tour).

Hansjorg Schmidt
Hansjorg Schmidt studied drama and theatre arts at Goldsmith's College and architectural lighting at the Bartlett School, University College London. He works as a freelance lighting designer for theatre, music and architecture, and teaches lighting design at Goldsmith's College. Recent work includes: *Henry VIII* (Bridewell Theatre, London); *A Perfect Ganesh* (Palace Theatre Watford); *Pal Joey* (Nottingham Playhouse and New Wolsey Theatre, Ipswich); *Around the World in 80 Days* (BAC, London). Hansjorg is resident lighting designer with Heart 'n Soul and lighting consultant for L'ouverture, a new arts centre on Trinity Buoy Wharf, London.

Alan Schofield
Starting with toy theatres, then church pantomimes and amateur dramatics, Alan Schofield has designed scenery since childhood. At 17 he secured a job as assistant to Sid Lane who designed and painted the gigantic outdoor sets for the historic fireworks dramas at Belle Vue, Manchester. A week before starting, Alan was made redundant and the productions were abandoned after running for 104 years. At that time the future for theatre scenery, particularly painted scenery, looked bleak. So for the next 30 years he made a career in photography and film making working as a designer, part time. In 1989 he became the first and only resident designer at the Elmhurst Ballet School where he stayed for six years before turning freelance, designing principally for pantomime and musicals. Since 1995 he has designed all the productions for the RTC (a rep company performing for children) at the Novello Theatre near Ascot. He is now working full time at the newly built Prospect Theatre at the Sixth Form College in Farnborough. Earlier this year he also became a director of Jubilee Productions recently formed to stage local youth and community theatre productions.

Nettie Scriven
Nettie Scriven has worked extensively throughout Britain and has a wealth of experience of theatre in a variety of spaces, including schools, community centres, studio theatres, art galleries and more traditional proscenium theatres. She specialises in creating new work, taking time to develop the piece with the writer and other collaborators, enabling the visual to inform the development of text, and vice versa. Her recent work includes *Aesop's Fables* (Sherman Theatre, Cardiff) and *The Secret Garden* (Nottingham Playhouse) and as visual artist on *In The Moment*, an inter-generational arts and video project (Nottinghamshire County Council). Selected previous work includes: *Stepper Joe* and *The Waltz* (West Yorkshire Playhouse); *The Lost Child* and *Plague of Innocence*, awarded 1988 Best Young People's Theatre Production (Crucible Theatre, Sheffield); *Hamlet* (Contact Theatre Manchester); *Crivelli's Garden* (Theatre Centre); *One for Sorrow* (Hijinx); *A Little Princess* (Yvonne Arnaud Theatre, Guildford); *The Snow Spider* (Sherman Theatre, Cardiff); *Rooms* (Glasshouses Dance Co); and *Between Friends* (Kommedia) which was part of the British exhibition at the 1999 Prague Quadrennial international exhibition of scenography. Nettie is a senior lecturer at Nottingham Trent

University using the disciplines of teaching and designing to enrich each other. She is on the board of directors at Theatre Centre, and is chair and a founder member of the Designers' Formation. She juggles her life as a designer and lecturer with motherhood.

Juliet Shillingford
Juliet Shillingford trained at Ravensbourne and Croydon Colleges of Art. She was awarded an Arts Council Bursary and then spent four years as a resident designer in Farnham and Manchester. She has been associated with the Nuffield Theatre, Southampton for a number of years and has had the privilege of designing for many new plays or UK premières, including *The Seduction of Anne Boleyn* by Claire Luckham, *Beach Wedding* and *Earth and Sky* which also did a national tour.
Most recently she designed *The Shagaround* by Maggie Neville also seen at the Soho Theatre and *Night Swimming* by Mark Castle, both products of the thriving Nuffield Theatre writers' group. She has designed several children's plays, among them *Jungle Book, Peter Pan* and *Alice in Wonderland*; also classics *Waiting for Godot* and *Rhinoceros*, all at the Nuffield. Other freelance work includes: *Piaf* and *Richard III* (Leicester Haymarket) and *The Fly* (Oldham Coliseum) - a co-design with her sister Felicity Shillingford. In the summer, Juliet frequently designs for workshop productions involving huge casts of various ages she has also taught at Richmond and Croydon Colleges of Art.

Tim Skelly
Tim Skelly is resident designer for the Workshop Theatre, Leeds University). He has also worked as a designer-in-residence at Bretton Hall and at the Royal Academy of Dramatic Art in London. As a freelance lighting designer his recent work includes: *Hijra* (West Yorkshire Playhouse); *Static, Clean, Neutrino* and *Safety* (Unlimited Theatre); *Brother Jacques* and *Union Street* (Plymouth Theatre Royal); *The Coming of Age Tour* (Janet Smith and Dancers); *Tosca* and *Nabucco* (Moldovan National Opera); *Korczak* (Teatr Muzyczny, Gdynia and Warsaw, Poland); *Having a Ball* (York Theatre Royal and Colchester Mercury); and *Plunge, Inside Somewhere, High Land* and *Daddy I'm Not Well* (Scottish Dance Theatre).
He has worked as a lighting consultant for Yorkshire Sculpture Park and has collaborated with several artists, including Sir Anthony Caro, Philip King and Christo. His academic interests lie in stage design for the theatre, with broader interests in 3D design for performance. Particular interests include the application of technologies in performance, lighting for dance theatre, light and sculpture, British theatre architecture (with a focus to the Victorian and Edwardian playhouse) and European scenography. He is contributing to a Leverhulme-funded project looking at Victorian Theatre in Leeds. He is studying the architecture of the Grand Theatre and Opera House, Leeds and placing this within a broader study of period theatres in the West Riding of Yorkshire. Using an award from the Arts and Humanities Research Board, he is undertaking a survey of key British lighting designers of the past 60 years.

Ian Sommerville
Ian Sommerville is a freelance set and lighting designer working mainly in the Opera House circuit around the world. He has also worked in theatre in the UK and as a fine artist has given several exhibitions of his work as a painter and installation artist. He is currently working towards a move into the film industry as a cinematographer with work planned in America and Italy. Look out for upcoming productions: *Miss Saigon*, for Malmö Musikteater and *After the Ball Was Over* at Dean Clough, Halifax.

Jessica Stack
Jessica Stack trained on the design course at the Bristol Old Vic Theatre School, having read drama at the University of Manchester. Theatre designs include: *The Blue Room, Confusions, Talking Heads, The Threepenny Opera, Blue Remembered Hills, Young Hearts* and *Kissing Sid James* (Hull Truck Theatre); *Fairytaleheart* (world première 1998) and *The Prince of West End Avenue* (world première 1997, Hampstead Theatre, London); *The Rape of Lucretia* (Royal Academy of Music); *Nicholas Nickleby* (Gateway Theatre, Chester); *Hamlet, Educating Rita and Pygmalion* (White Horse Theatre, Germany); *Don Quixote* (Salisbury Playhouse Youth Theatre); *Torch Song Trilogy* and *Mrs Warren's Profession* (Eye Theatre, Suffolk); and *The Filibuster* (world première 1998, Tristan Bates Theatre, London). She designed the live broadcast of *Wembley Stadium Auction* (Skysports and IbidLive). Jessica also designs corporate events. These have include events for ?WhatIf! in London and France (clients include BBC and Unilever), and for Lane Group at Centre Parcs.

Andrew Storer
Andrew Storer studied theatre design at Wimbledon School of Art. He began his career designing productions for London Contemporary Dance Theatre and Ballet Rambert. He has created over 30 designs for the choreographer Robert North, including the full-length ballets *Elvira Madigan* (Royal Danish Ballet); *Romeo and Juliet* and *Offenbach* (Grand Théâtre Geneva, Arena di Verona and Scottish Ballet); *Living in America, Love, Life and Death, Russian Story* and *Eva* (Gothenburg Opera). Other recent productions include *Petrouchka* (Grand Théâtre de Bordeaux) *Short Cuts* (Arena di Verona), *Bach Dances* (Semperoper, Dresden) and *The Snowman* (Scottish Ballet).
Andrew has created designs for the choreographers Christopher Bannerman, Mark Morris and Wayne Sleep as well as working extensively in Europe designing many ballet and opera productions for companies including English National Ballet, Hanover Opera, Stuttgart Ballet, Théâtre du Capitole Toulouse, Teatro dell'Opera Rome, Teatro San Carlo Naples, Spoleto Festival, Ballet Toscana Florence and Teatro Regio Turin. His designs for television include the award-winning ballet *For My Daughter* (Danish Royal Ballet/Danish TV) and *Lonely Town, Lonely Street* (Ballet Rambert/Virgin Classic Video). He has also designed the lighting for *Tryst*, by James MacMillan (Scottish Chamber Orchestra/BBC1), the *Sound Bites Two* series with Evelyn Glennie (BBC Scottish Symphony Orchestra/ BBC2); and *Red Forecast* by Tan Dun (BBC Scottish Symphony Orchestra/BBC2).

Nancy Surman
Nancy Surman's recent work includes: designs for the stage première of *My Beautiful Laundrette* (SNAP Theatre Company); major tours of *Aspects of Love* and *Noel and Gertie* (Gordon Craig Theatre, Stevenage); *The Duchess of Malfi* and *The Rivals* (Salisbury Playhouse); and *Beautiful Thing* (Oxfordshire Touring Theatre Company). She designed the world premières of *Rock & Roll* and *Barbirolli* (Snap Theatre Company); *The Road to Hell* and *Johnny Watkins Walks on Water* (Birmingham Rep) and *A Stinging Sea (Citizens' Theatre, Glasgow). Other productions include: The Secret Rapture, Rough Crossing* and *The Winter's Tale* (Salisbury Playhouse); *Talent* (Mercury Theatre, Colchester and Palace Theatre, Watford); *Kaahini* and *Bonded* (Birmingham Rep); new adaptations of *Sons and Lovers, Pride and Prejudice, Tom Jones, Far from the Madding Crowd* and *Maurice* (SNAP Theatre Company); *The Hunchback of Notre Dame, He Said, She Said* and *Don Quixote* (Oxfordshire Touring Theatre Company); *The Final Appearance of Miss Mamie Stuart* and *Stepping Out* (Torch Theatre); *Laurel and Hardy* (Cheltenham Everyman).

David I Taylor
David I Taylor trained in theatre design at London University and the University of Massachusetts. Recent lighting designs include: a new production of *The Lady's not for Burning* (San José Repertory Theatre) and the London première of *The Mai* (Tricycle Theatre). In New York, he designed the new musical *Shabbatai* and the New York première of *The Workroom* for American Jewish Theatre.
Other notable productions include *Macbeth*, lit by fire and flame for Nicholas Kent; the première of *Walpurgis Night* (Gate Theatre, London) and the acclaimed production of *Gamblers*, designed by Oleg Sheintsis (Tricycle Theatre). Other recent work includes a London production of *Chicago*; *Le nozze di Figaro* (Stowe); *Sir Thomas More* (Shaw Theatre); a new production of Nick Ward's *The Strangeness of Others*, and a tour of the song and dance show *Sleep with Friends* with Wayne Sleep. He designed lights for the première of *Dreyfus* (London), the double bill *Wine in the Wilderness* and *Water*, and a new production of *Little Shop of Horrors* in New York. David is a director of Theatre Projects Consultants and was consultant for the new home of the Philadelphia Orchestra, the new home for the Academy Awards.

Ian Teague
Ian Teague trained at Trent Polytechnic (now The Nottingham Trent University). He started work in 1982 as assistant designer at the Liverpool Everyman Theatre. His design projects include main-house rep shows, community plays, small scale touring, TIE, YPT and youth theatre. He has been involved in over 100 productions. The past four years have seen an increasing integration of IT into his working methods. A visiting lecturer in set design at Middlesex University and in IT in the design process at Central School of Speech and Drama. He has been a member of the Equity Designers Committee since 1990. He has his own web site where you can see examples of his work. This can be found at www.geocities.com/iteague.

Yannis Thavoris
Yannis Thavoris was born in Thessaloniki, Greece. He is the winner of the 1997 Linbury Prize for Stage Design. In 1994 he graduated with a diploma from the School of Architecture at the Aristotle University of Thessaloniki. He was awarded the Lilian Voudouris Foundation scholarship in Athens to study at Central Saint Martin's College of Art and Design, where he graduated with a Master of Arts in European Scenography in 1997. Yannis has worked in opera, theatre and architecture. His recent designs for sets and costume include: Britten's *The Rape of Lucretia* (Aldeburgh Festival, ENO and BBC TV) and Puccini's *Madama Butterfly* (Scottish Opera) both directed by David McVicar; *The Rake's Progress* (ENO); Bizet's *Carmen* (English Touring Opera); Puccini's *Tosca* (Surrey Opera); Ian Spink's production of Donizetti's *The Daughter of The Regiment* (English Touring Opera); Michael Bogdanov's production of *Antony and Cleopatra* (English Shakespeare Company) and Wedekind's *Franziska* (The Gate Theatre, London). His work in architecture includes collaborating on the design of a 300-seat theatre auditorium and the restoration of a 19th-century industrial complex.

Johanna Town
Johanna Town began her theatre career in 1980 at the Royal Exchange Theatre, Manchester, where she was so inspired by the use of lighting in the round she pursued a career as lighting designer. She was resident lighting designer at the Liverpool Playhouse in the late 1980s, where she lit over 20 productions. In 1990 she became head of lighting at Royal Court Theatre. Credits there include: *The Kitchen, Faith Healer, Search and Destroy, Pale Horse, Mr Kolpert, I Just Stopped By To See The Man, Plastercine, Where Do We Live, Other People.* In 1996 she became the lighting consultant for the design and refurbishment of the new Jerwood theatres at the Royal Court. Her freelance career has allowed her to design over a dozen productions for Out of Joint and tour these productions world wide. They include: *Rita Sue & Bob Too/A State Affair, Some Explicit Polaroids, Our Country's Good, Blue Heart* and *Three Sisters.* Other theatre credits include: *Rose, Arabian Nights, Steward of Christendom, Shopping & Fucking* (New York); *Feelgood, Top Girls, Beautiful Thing, Little Malcolm and his struggle against the Eunuchs* (London West End); *Hinterland, Our Lady of Sligo* (National Theatre); *Popcorn, Les Liaisons Dangereuses, Playboy of the Western World* (Liverpool Playhouse); *Ghosts, The Misfits, The Lodger* (Royal Exchange Theatre). Opera credits include: *Tobias and the Angel* (Almeida Festival); *The Marriage of Figaro, Otello* (Nice Opera House); *La Bohème, Die Fledermaus, La Traviata, The Magic Flute* (Music Theatre London); *Abduction from the Seraglio, The Marriage of Figaro* (Opera 80).

Mayou Trikerioti
Mayou Trikerioti trained at the Bristol Old Vic Theatre School (postgraduate theatre design 1999-2000), and the

University of Kent (BA Hons in drama and theatre studies, specialising in design 1995-1999). She has also followed short courses in costume and fine art at Central St Martin's and the London School of Fashion (2000-2001). Credits include: set and costumes for *What Where, The Dumb Waiter, The Lover, Cage Birds, The Pear Tree* (all at the Lumley Studio, Canterbury); *Scapin* (Gulbenkian Theatre, Canterbury); *The Bespoke Overcoat, Mild Oats* (Old Vic Basement, Bristol); *Hospital, The Travel Agent* (Tunbridge Wells); *The Professional* (Teatro Technis, Athens); *Silence and Violence* (White Bear, London); *Not I* (for the Cultural Olympics, Athens); *Winter* (Amore Theatre, Athens). Costumes for: *Under Milk Wood* (New Vic, Bristol). Sets for: *Equus* (Lumley Studio, Canterbury); *School For Scandal* (Redgrave Theatre, Bristol); *The Interview* (Cockpit Theatre, London); *Fairly Tales* (UK tour, including the Gate, London, and the Edinburgh Fringe Festival); *Return to the Forbidden Planet* (St George's Square Theatre, Edinburgh); *Lulu* (Theatro Athinais, Athens).

Katy Tuxford
Katy Tuxford studied theatre design at Nottingham Trent University. While there she designed *Macbeth* in conjunction with Nottingham Playhouse. After graduating, she worked at The Mill at Sonning Theatre, designing *Outside Edge, Sylvia's Wedding* and *Relatively Speaking*. Freelance work includes: *Ruffian on the Stair* and *Funeral Games* (Pentameters Theatre, London); *Eclipsed* (Riverside Studios, London); and work with Streets Alive Theatre Company (London and Ghana). Seven shows for Stagedoor Manor, New York include *Playing for Time, Merrily We Roll Along, 42nd Street* and *The Boyfriend*. Other designs include: *The Wordsmith's Lament, Daydream Believer, A Slice of Saturday Night, How the Other Half Loves, Duck Variations* and *Squirrels* (Upstairs at the Gatehouse); *Sweet Charity* (Watford Palace); *Macbeth* (Cambridge Arts); *Severance* (Palace Theatre Westcliff). Film work, as production designer: *Parasite* (Fearnort Films). Television: *The Forsyte Saga* (Granada TV).

Joe Vaněk
Joe Vaněk trained for theatre design with an MA at Manchester University. He then worked as head of design at various British regional theatres in the 1970s and 1980s. He first worked in Ireland with director Patrick Mason in 1984, moving to Dublin in 1994 to become director of design for Ireland's National Theatre, the Abbey.
Since 1998 he has been working freelance. In Ireland, he has designed world premières of many leading Irish playwrights, the most famous of which, *Dancing at Lughnasa*, by Brian Friel, was subsequently presented at the National Theatre, in the West End and on Broadway, where he received two Tony Award nominations. In the USA (in San José) he has designed Marina Carr's *By the Bog of Cats* with Holly Hunter. During the past 15 years he has designed a wide range of operas including: *Don Pasquale, Ariane and Bluebeard* (Opera North); *Il Trittico* (ENO); *Rigoletto* (Welsh National Opera); and *The Love for Three Oranges* (Royal Danish Opera).
In Ireland, his designs have been seen at the Wexford Festival (1987 and 1989) and for major productions for Opera Theatre Company and Opera Ireland. In 1997 he designed the national tour of Cliff Richard's *Heathcliff*. In marked contrast he has recently worked with American film director, Neil Labute on his play *b.a.s.h.* In 1998 he designed his first full-length ballet, *Legs of Fire*, based on the film of *The Red Shoes*, for the Royal Danish Ballet and was recently reunited with its choreographer Flemming Flindt for *The Triumph of Death* which opened in Copenhagen in October 2002.

Jamie Vartan
Jamie Vartan trained at Central Saint Martin's School of Art and Design, London. He was awarded an Arts Council Bursary to work at Nottingham Playhouse. He was involved for three years as designer and artist-in-residence with the David Glass Ensemble on *The Lost Child Trilogy*, which included residencies involving workshops, research and new devised productions in Vietnam, Indonesia, China, the Philippines and Colombia. *The Trilogy* was later presented at the Young Vic and he also created an installation at the October Gallery, London, based on the work from the overseas residencies. At the National Theatre of Ireland (The Abbey and Peacock Theatres) he has designed *Blackwater Angel, The Playboy of The Western World, The Hostage, A Little Like Paradise, Sour Grapes, Making History* and *Mrs Warren's Profession* (nomination for *Irish Times* Theatre Awards Best Production).
Other theatre work includes *Nosferatu the Visitor* (Red Shift Theatre Company) and *Because It's There* (Nottingham Playhouse). Current work in opera includes *La Traviata* (Malmö Musikteater, Sweden). Other designs for opera include *A Village Romeo and Juliet* (Teatro Lirico di Cagliari, Sardinia), *The Dwarf* (Teatro Comunale, Florence and Teatro Regio, Turin). Design for dance with choreographer Darshan Singh Bhuller includes *Recall* (Linbury Studio, Royal Opera, Covent Garden and UK tour), and a new production for Phoenix Dance Company (Sadler's Wells and UK tour). Design for film includes *Paradise Fish Bar* (BBC), *Smell* (Munich and Angers Film Festival Awards). He was art director for *The King of Jazz* (BBC).

Janet Vaughan
Janet Vaughan trained in theatre design at Nottingham Trent Polytechnic and now works as a freelance artist and designer utilising a variety of media. She has designed site-specific and touring film and theatre works, and created artworks for gallery, non-gallery, unusual and outdoor spaces. She is one third of Coventry's acclaimed Talking Birds, most recently designing the company's site-specific show trial *Solid Blue*, for a 14th-century monastery next to the Coventry ring road flyover, and *Hypnogogia*, an elegy to a city, in two halves of 15 minutes with a two-hour interval. Her design for Talking Birds' *Smoke, Mirrors & the Art of Escapology* formed part of the British entry to the 1999 Prague Quadrennial. Janet also designs and maintains the company's award-winning website 'innovative and unusual... akin to taking part in a David Lynch movie' (*The Independent*) at www.talkingbirds.co.uk. She is particularly interested in the integration of moving images and projection within live spaces, and her site-specific work reflects her interest in the relationship between art and the environment in which it is created and viewed. As one half of Artists In Waiting, she was artist in residence in six of Coventry City Council's public waiting areas, producing six new site-specific artworks as part of the national Year of the Artist in 2001.

Juliet Watkinson
Juliet Wilkinson trained on the ENO Design Course and has worked mainly in repertory theatre. Apart from freelance design work, her two longer-term residencies have been at the Abbey Theatre, Dublin and the Gateway Theatre, Chester. During the past four years (the scope of this exhibition),she has been working largely in the field of education.
With the Cheshire Drama Advisory Service, she has designed and facilitated large-scale county youth productions, and devised workshops and design experiences for young people and teachers. She has worked for theatre in education and community theatre companies such as Action Transport and MC. She has designed for students at the Arden School of Theatre, Manchester and worked with undergraduates and graduates from Chester College. She has found the range of her work extremely exciting - especially since it has often involved working in non-theatre spaces and working in a collaborative way with students, young people and other professionals and specialists.
She endeavours to share the excitement of design and creativity as well as trying to promote the rigorous reality of a professional approach to making these creative ideas actually happen for any given production.

Fiona Watt
Fiona trained with Motley. Her ambition to train as a designer was encouraged by the Royal Court Young People's Theatre, a formative experience which continues to influence her working relationships today. She finds inspiration in each writer's unique use of language, endeavouring to create environments that capture the essence of the piece while allowing actors space to tell stories. Theatre credits include: *Outlying Islands* by David Greig (Edinburgh Festival); *The Trestle at Pope Lick Creek* by Naomi Wallace; *Heritage* by Nicola McCartney, and *Highland Shorts* for the Traverse Theatre (Edinburgh). Opera credits include: *La Traviata* for Haddo House Opera; *Mavra, Riders to the Sea, Gianni Schicchi* and *La Pietra del Paragone* for Royal Scottish Academy of Music and Drama. She has also designed for the Sherman Theatre, Cardiff, Palace Theatre Watford, Eastern Angles, Paines Plough and extensively in Theatre in Education for companies such as Nottingham Roundabout, TAG, Yorkshire Women Theatre, Theatr Clywd and the Tricycle Theatre, London. In 1996 she was awarded an Arts Council of England Design Bursary, allowing her to be based at the Wolsey Theatre, Ipswich. She has exhibited her work in *Time + Space* (Royal College of Art,London) and at the Tron Theatre, Glasgow, as part of the UK City of Architecture and Design. She is represented by The Designers Formation.

Naomi Wilkinson
Naomi Wilkinson trained at the Motley Theatre Design Course after a BA Hons in fine art at the University of the West of England. In recent years she has worked regularly with the physical theatre company Told by an Idiot. Productions have included: *I weep at my Piano* (Newcastle Gulbenkian); *Happy Birthday Mr Deka D* (Traverse Theatre); *Shoot Me in the Heart* (Gate Theatre); *Aladdin* (Lyric Theatre Hammersmith); and most recently *I Can't Wake Up* (Lyric Theatre Studio). Other credits include: *Mules, My Life in the Bush of Ghosts* and *Heredity* (all Royal Court Theatre); *It's Only a Game Show* (First Person Dance); *Gobbledygook* (Gogmagogs, Traverse Theatre/New York tour); *The Prince of Homberg* (National Theatre Studio); *Well Farewell* and *Witch Hunt* (Brouhaha, UK tour); *Two Horsemen* (Gate and Bush Theatres, *Time Out* and London New Play Festival awards); *Snake House* (Greenwich Studio, London); *Suicide & Manipulation* (Finborough Theatre, London); *In Pursuit of a Dream* (Purcell Room, London). For television: *The Loser* (Channel 4). Future projects include: *Arcane* for Opera Circus and *A Little Fantasy* for Told by an Idiot.

Simon Wilkinson
Simon Wilkinson studied at Edinburgh University where he lit many shows for the resident company at the Bedlam Theatre. Following this he has worked in corporate and event lighting, as well as theatre design. Theatre designs include: *Illyria* (Scottish Youth Theatre, Eden Court); *Spoonface Steinberg* (Manick Company and Queen Margaret University College); *Mum's The Word* (Robert C Kelly Ltd & CCE, Scottish tour); *A Christmas Carol* (Byre Theatre); *Ghost Shirt* (Theatre by Design); *Lion in the Streets* (Arches Theatre); *Stories in Harmony* (INfusion Festival); *Better Days ... Better Knights* (Fifth Estate); *Last Supper of Dr Faustus* (Fringe First Award Winner). He has also lit a range of music and musicals, including: *Touch Bass* (Arches Theatre); *Always ... Patsy Cline* (national tour); *In Town Tonight* and *Dean Park's Big Night Out* (King's Theatre, Edinburgh and King's Theatre, Glasgow); and Scotland's last surviving summer season variety show, *The Gaiety Whirl*. He was the lighting designer for the Guinness World Record winning production of *Oklahoma!* at the Edinburgh Playhouse when Act 24 staged this musical from scratch in under 24 hours.

Bryan Willams
Bryan Williams began his career in retail display and design management for the John Lewis Partnership. Subsequently he returned to his heartland in the north of England where he co-established the award-winning Northern Theatre Company, now in its 27th year. As a mature student, he studied three-dimensional design at Humberside University. Both during his studies and since graduation, he has created and supervised the construction of over a 100 theatrical sets for his and other theatre companies, such as Hull Truck.
Much of his work was for original scripts, requiring him to become involved with the authors and directors at the earliest moments of the creative process, often before a word was written. Bryan devotes part of his time

to lecturing in higher education to help young designers get a start in their careers. A number of former students now work in theatre and television.

Keith Williams Architects

Keith R Williams, BA (Hons), DipArch (Hons), RIBA, was educated at Kingston and Greenwich Schools of Architecture. He worked first for Sheppard Robson and then Terry Farrell before founding Pawson Williams Architects in 1987 and establishing it as a major player in the design of buildings for the arts. In January 2001, he formed Keith Williams Architects in order to concentrate on the development of a singular creative approach to architecture against a background of an expanding portfolio of high profile commissions in the UK and abroad. His architecture, with its concerns for space, light, form and material, consistently exhibits a close consideration for scale, history and context, thereby achieving an aesthetic balance between his own contemporary, visionary architecture and that which exists, whether sensitive and historic or 'brownfield'. He has a particular interest in the performing arts and in the spaces in which they take place. He has been on the assessment panels for major public projects. He has judged national design awards and won national and international architectural competitions. He also teaches and lectures and his work has been published worldwide. The firm's many buildings and projects include: Unicorn Theatre for Children, London; the redevelopment of Birmingham Repertory Theatre; the Mercat Arts Centre, Dingwall; New City Library and Performing Arts Centre, Torino; Nieztsche Museum & Archive, Naumburg, Germany; Literatur Museum, Marbach am Neckar, Germany; the Earth Galleries redevelopment at the Natural History Museum; masterplan for Museum der Bildendenkünst, Leipzig; town hall and library, Athlone, Republic of Ireland; Copenhagen Philharmonic Hall; the CRMV Performing Arts Complex, Paris.

Sue Willmington

Sue Willmington gained a BA Hons in fine art before studying post graduate theatre design at Motley. Plays include: *The Beaux' Stratagem* (National Theatre); *The Liar* (Old Vic, London); *A Midsummer Night's Dream* (Zurich); *All For Love* (Almeida Theatre, London); *Fortune's Fool* (Chichester); *Measure For Measure, The White Devil, The Merchant of Venice, Don Carlos, Richard II, Love in a Wood* (RSC). Operas include: *Tosca, A Masked Ball* (Hong Kong Arts Festival); *Nabucco, Fidelio, Porgy and Bess* (Bregenz Festival); *Maria Stuarda, Dalibor* (Scottish Opera); *Seraglio* (Strasbourg); *Eugene Onegin, Genoveva* (Opera North); *Simon Boccanegra* (Welsh National Opera and Strasbourg); *Carmen, Rigoletto, Lucia di Lammermoor* (New Israeli Opera); *La fancuilla del West, Don Carlos, Die schweigsame Frau* (Zurich); *La Clemenza di Tito* (Dallas Opera and Royal Opera, Covent Garden); *Capriccio* (Turin). Musical theatre credits include: *Anything Goes* (Grange Park Opera); *Show Time at the Stadium* (BBC Wales); *Scrooge* (Tokyo); associate costume designer on *Jesus Christ Superstar* (London).

Louise Ann Wilson

Louise Ann Wilson graduated with a first class BA (Hons) in theatre design from Nottingham Trent University and was a Linbury Prize exhibitor in 1993. She was the British representative of Theatre Designers Working for Audiences of Young People at the 'Assitej' International Seminar, Prague Quadrennial, 1995. She is the co-artistic director of Wilson&Wilson Company. The company (WWCo) creates site-specific theatre with artists from different disciplines. In 2002 she co-created/designed *Mapping the Edge*, a WWCo and Sheffield Crucible co-production, which took its audience on a journey via bus, tram and on foot to various locations around the city of Sheffield. In *House* (Huddersfield Contemporary Music Festival, 1998) the company transformed two 19th-century workers cottages into an extraordinary performance space. WWCo are now creating *Crossing the Gobi*, a theatre/opera production inspired by the cities of Leeds, UK, and Chengdu, China. It will be performed in both cities in 2003. Louise works as a freelance designer in theatre, opera and dance. She has recently designed productions for: Opera North, Sheffield Crucible, West Yorkshire Playhouse, Theatre Centre, the Sherman Theatre, Unicorn Theatre, Strathcona Theatre, Lip Service, The Watermill Theatre, Lawrence Batley Theatre, The Gate (London), Chelsea Centre, Live Theatre and award-winning productions for Manchester Royal Exchange and Midsommer Actors. She created the multi-media installation *Under the Roofs* of Paris to accompany Opera North's *Amaze Me* season at the Town Hall in Leeds.

Andrew Wood

Andrew Wood studied theatre design at Nottingham Trent Polytechnic and graduated in 1991. He worked as a freelance designer before joining Contact Theatre in Manchester where, over five years, he filled every position in the design department from assistant to associate director (design). Designs for Contact include *Romeo and Juliet, A Midsummer Night's Dream, The Trial*, the touring production of *The Mill on the Floss* and six Young Playwrights Festivals. Since returning to freelance work designs have included: *Neville's Island* and *Blithe Spirit* (Harrogate Theatre); *Cold* and The Barramundi Festival (The Ashton Group Contemporary Theatre); the Future Tense and Northern Lines Festivals (New Writing North and Live Theatre in Newcastle); and *To You*, which was the opening production at the Lowry Centre, Salford. More recently he has designed *Oleanna* for Hull Truck and *52 Degrees South* for Big Theatre at the newly opened Imperial War Museum North, in Manchester. Andrew is a part-time lecturer in performance design at the Arden School of Theatre in Manchester and has worked as a visiting lecturer at the Liverpool Institute for Performing Arts and Manchester Metropolitan and Salford Universities.

Haibo Yu

Haibo Yu trained at the Central Academy of Drama in China where he also executed a number of designs for theatre and television. He won a scholarship to study at the University of Leeds in 1986 and then transferred to a postgraduate course in scenography at Central Saint Martin's College of Art and Design in London. His designs have been widely seen in theatre, film and television, including theatre designs: *Bright Angel* and *Babble* (Proteus Theatre Company, tour); *Whale* (Harrogate Theatre); and *Stone Angels* (Bloomsbury Theatre, London). Films: *Foreign Moon* (Media Asia, Hong Kong); *The Opium War* (UK locations, Xie Jin Films, Shanghai). Television: *The Historic Turning Point* (Transatlantic Films, London). Haibo currently teaches Scenography in USA.

Index of productions

134

Index of designers

Index of companies